NO LONGER PROPERTY OF
SEATTLE PUBLIC LIBRARY

D1164811

Eyewitness
Evolution

Snails with feelers extended
Skull of early hominid *Homo erectus*
Rock containing fossilized remains of several species of trilobite
Duck-billed platypus
Fossilized skeleton of *Procynosuchus*, a mammal-like reptile
Skull of modern human
Rock composed of millions of seashells

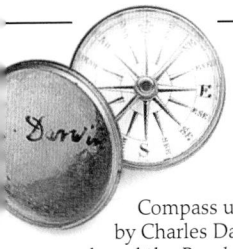

Compass used by Charles Darwin aboard the *Beagle*

Butterfly wing from Charles Darwin's collection

Eyewitness Evolution

Written by
LINDA GAMLIN

Froglets

South American *Agrias claudina* butterfly

Bee orchid

DK Publishing

LONDON, NEW YORK,
MELBOURNE, MUNICH, AND DELHI

Project editor Ian Whitelaw
Art editor Jane Bull
Designer Marianna Papachrysanthou
Production Adrian Gathercole
Managing editor Josephine Buchanan
Senior art editor Thomas Keenes
Picture research Deborah Pownall, Catherine O'Rourke
Special photography Andy Crawford, Neil Fletcher, Steve Gorton, Dave King, Harry Taylor
Editorial consultant Professor J Maynard Smith, University of Sussex
US Editor Charles A. Wills
US consultant Professor O. Roger Anderson, Columbia University

Revised Edition
Consultant Douglas Palmer
Editors Jayne Miller, Steve Setford
Art editors Edward Kinsey, Peter Radcliffe
Managing editor Camilla Hallinan
Managing art editor Owen Peyton Jones
Art director Martin Wilson
Associate publisher Andrew Macintyre
Production Laragh Kedwell, Pip Tinsley
Picture research Myriam Megharbi

This Eyewitness ® Guide has been conceived by Dorling Kindersley Limited and Editions Gallimard

First published in the United States in 1993
This revised edition published in 2009 by
DK Publishing, 375 Hudson Street, New York, New York 10014

Copyright © 1993, © 2009 Dorling Kindersley Limited

09 10 11 12 13 10 9 8 7 6 5 4 3 2
ED769 – 03/09

All rights reserved under International and Pan-American Copyright Conventions. No part of this publication may be reproduced, stored in a retrieval system, or transmitted in any form or by any means, electronic, mechanical, photocopying, recording or otherwise, without the prior written permission of the copyright owner. Published in Great Britain by Dorling Kindersley Limited.

A catalog record for this book is available from the Library of Congress

ISBN 978-0-7566-5028-5 (HC); 978-0-7566-5029-2 (ALB)

Color reproduction by Colourscan, Singapore
Printed by Toppan Co., (Shenzen) Ltd., China

Discover more at
www.dk.com

"Hand" and "finger" bones of horse's leg

19th-century microscope

Beetl

Bones of armadillo's forelimb

Bones of dolphin's flipper

Contents

Members of the insect order Hemiptera

6
Creation stories
8
Fossils and fairy tales
10
Victims of the flood
12
Jean-Baptiste de Lamarck
14
Extinct animals
16
A series of catastrophes
18
Dinosaur frenzy
20
Charles Darwin
22
Living evidence
24
Animal and plant distribution
26
Fossil evidence
28
How old is Earth?
30
Artificial selection
32
Variation and inheritance
34
The struggle for existence
36
Natural selection
38
Understanding adaptation
40
How new species are formed
42
Living intermediates
44
Fossil intermediates
46
Jumps and gaps
48
Ladders and branches
50
Gregor Mendel
52
Solving the DNA puzzle
54
The molecular evidence
56
The origin of life
58
Science and belief
60
History of life
62
Up to the present
64
Classifying life
66
Discoveries in Evolution
68
Find out more
70
Glossary
72
Index

Creation stories

WHERE DO PEOPLE COME FROM? How did the world begin? Where do plants and animals come from? People have been thinking about these questions for thousands of years, and there are many answers in the form of traditional stories. Some of these stories tell of a god who created the world and everything in it, including people. Other stories have many gods, who each made different things and then fought great battles for control of the world. Not all stories describe the world as having been created, however. Some tell of the world growing out of nothing, or out of chaos, without any creator. According to Buddhist beliefs, there was no beginning: instead, the universe goes through endless cycles of being and nonbeing. The stories are all very different, but they often try to explain certain things about life. Some explain why people get sick and die, or why there is night and day. They may also explain some minor features of living things, such as why snakes have no legs. More importantly, the stories often give people rules or guidelines for their lives. They may say something about the different ways in which men and women should behave, or how people should treat the animals and plants around them. Many religious authorities regard these stories as valuable lessons on how people should live, rather than factual accounts of how life on Earth actually began.

IN THE BEGINNING
These 16th-century illustrations show the Biblical creation story, which Christians and Jews share. There are two versions of the story, both in the first book of the Bible, Genesis. In the first version, shown here, man and woman are made simultaneously on the sixth day of creation. In the second version of the story, God creates the first man, Adam, before any other living thing. He then plants the Garden of Eden and makes all the animals. His final act is to create the first woman, Eve.

CREATORS OF THE WORLD
The Japanese creation story tells th in the beginning there were eight gods. When the youngest two, Izanagi and Izanami, stirred the ocean with a jeweled spear, falling drops of water formed an island. They came to live there and Izanami gave birth to all the islands of Japan.

HATCHED FROM AN EGG
This carving of a bird-headed god holding an egg comes from Easter Island in the Pacific Ocean. Here tradition says that the first people hatched from eggs laid by birds. On other Pacific islands, people were said to have hatched from turtles' eggs, or from rocks.

MAKER OF HUMANKIND
Carved by the people of Rurutu Island in the Pacific, this statue of the god Tangaroa is covered in tiny people that he has created. The same god appears in myths from other Pacific islands, but in some of these he is just one god among many and not the creator.

nans ng to roa's body

FROM THE FIRE
In addition to the great creation stories, there have always been minor legends explaining the origins of plants and animals. In Europe, salamanders were said to be born from flames. Salamanders do hide among damp logs and may have been seen rushing out from the flames of log fires.

Illustration from the Middle Ages, showing a salamander rising from the flames

EXPLAINING THE WORLD
The Biblical Genesis story explains, among other things, why snakes have no legs. God forbade Adam and Eve to eat from the tree of knowledge of good and evil, but a serpent tempted Eve to eat the fruit. As a punishment, the serpent was told: "Upon thy belly shalt thou go and dust shalt thou eat."

DEADLY SCREAM
In Europe, one minor legend concerned the mandrake plant, whose roots are sometimes human-shaped. The legend claimed that mandrake roots cried out when pulled from the ground, and this shriek would kill anyone who heard it. This pagan belief survived into Christian times.

naginative medieval oodcut of the andrake plant

CHANGING FORMS
Stalked barnacles are often seen attached to driftwood. In medieval times, they were said to grow on trees and then to turn into barnacle geese that flew away. Scientific study of the living world, from the 16th century on, cast doubts on such legends, and careful observation gradually took their place.

Medieval drawing of barnacle goose "tree"

Stalked barnacles on driftwood

Fossils and fairy tales

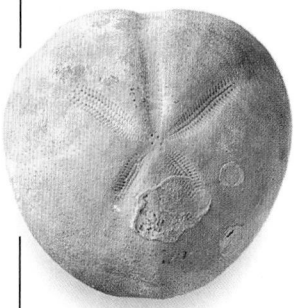

ELFIN FARE
Thinking they were fairy loaves, people in southern England kept fossil heart urchins like this in their pantries to ensure that there would always be bread for the family.

FOSSILS ARE THE REMAINS or impressions of living things hardened in rock. People have been finding fossils for at least 30,000 years. Ice Age hunters made them into necklaces, and the idea that fossils had magical properties may well have begun then. Magical beliefs about fossils became common all over the world. The Chinese kept tiny fossilized fish in their food pantries to keep away insect pests called silverfish. The Roman scholar Pliny the Elder wrote that fossilized sea urchins could cure snakebites and ensure success in battle. He also collected some extraordinary "tall tales" to explain the origins of fossils: sea urchin fossils were said to be formed from balls of foam created by masses of entwined snakes. Other people developed theories to explain fossils in general. One idea was that the rain picked up the seeds and eggs of living things from the sea. When the rain fell and seeped into rocks, the seeds and eggs grew into stony replicas of their true selves. This was an attempt to explain why so many fossils are clearly sea creatures. A more fanciful theory, popular from medieval times until the 17th century, was that Earth had its own "creative force," or *vis plastica*, and this force was trying to make copies of living things.

Fossil mold

Dr. Plc horseli illustrati of the fos

STONE HORSES
This unusual fossil is the cast, or mold, of the inside of a shell called *Myophorella*. The shell itself has dissolved away. The living animal was similar to an oyster, having two shells held together by a strong muscle. This left a circular mark on each side, and Dr. Robert Plot (1640–1696) interpreted these as eyes. With great imagination, he also saw two ears and a mane and declared that this was an attempt by Earth's *vis plastica* to make a horse's head.

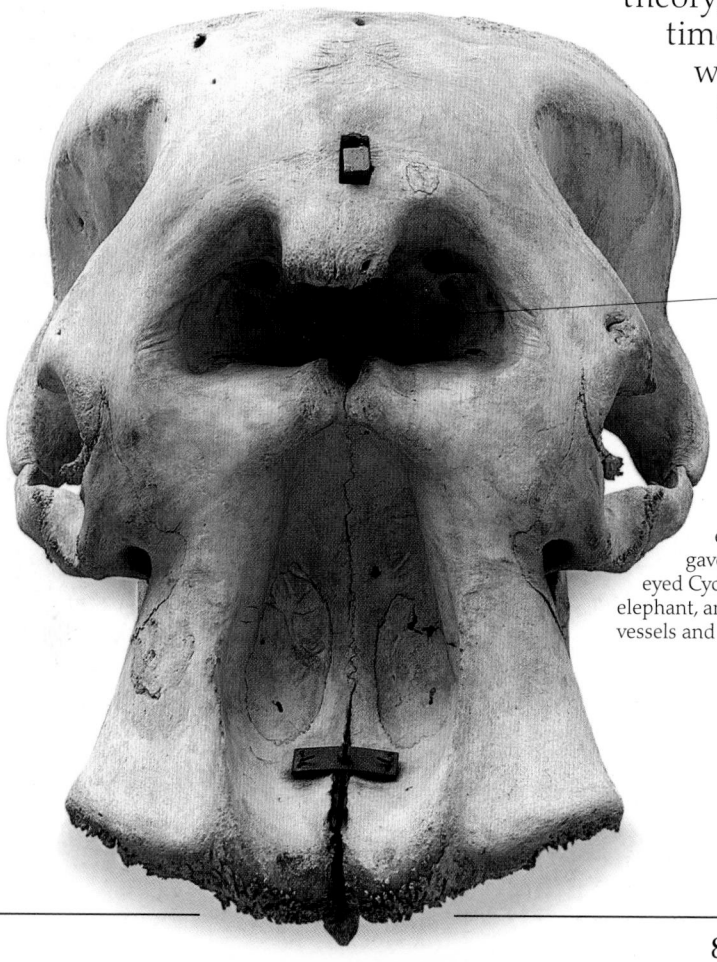

Opening in skull for trunk

ONE-EYED MAN
When skulls like this were found in fossil form on the Mediterranean island of Sicily, the ancient Greeks imagined giant men, each with a single eye in his forehead. This belief gave rise to the legend of the one-eyed Cyclops. In fact, this is the skull of an elephant, and the hole is where its blood vessels and airways ran down to the trunk.

BLINDING THE GIANT
On a vase from ancient Greece, the hero Odysseus is shown blinding the Cyclops Polyphemus with an iron brand as he sleeps in his cave on Mount Aetna in Sicily. Odysseus and his companions were able to escape from the island but made an enemy of Poseidon the sea god, the father of the Cyclops.

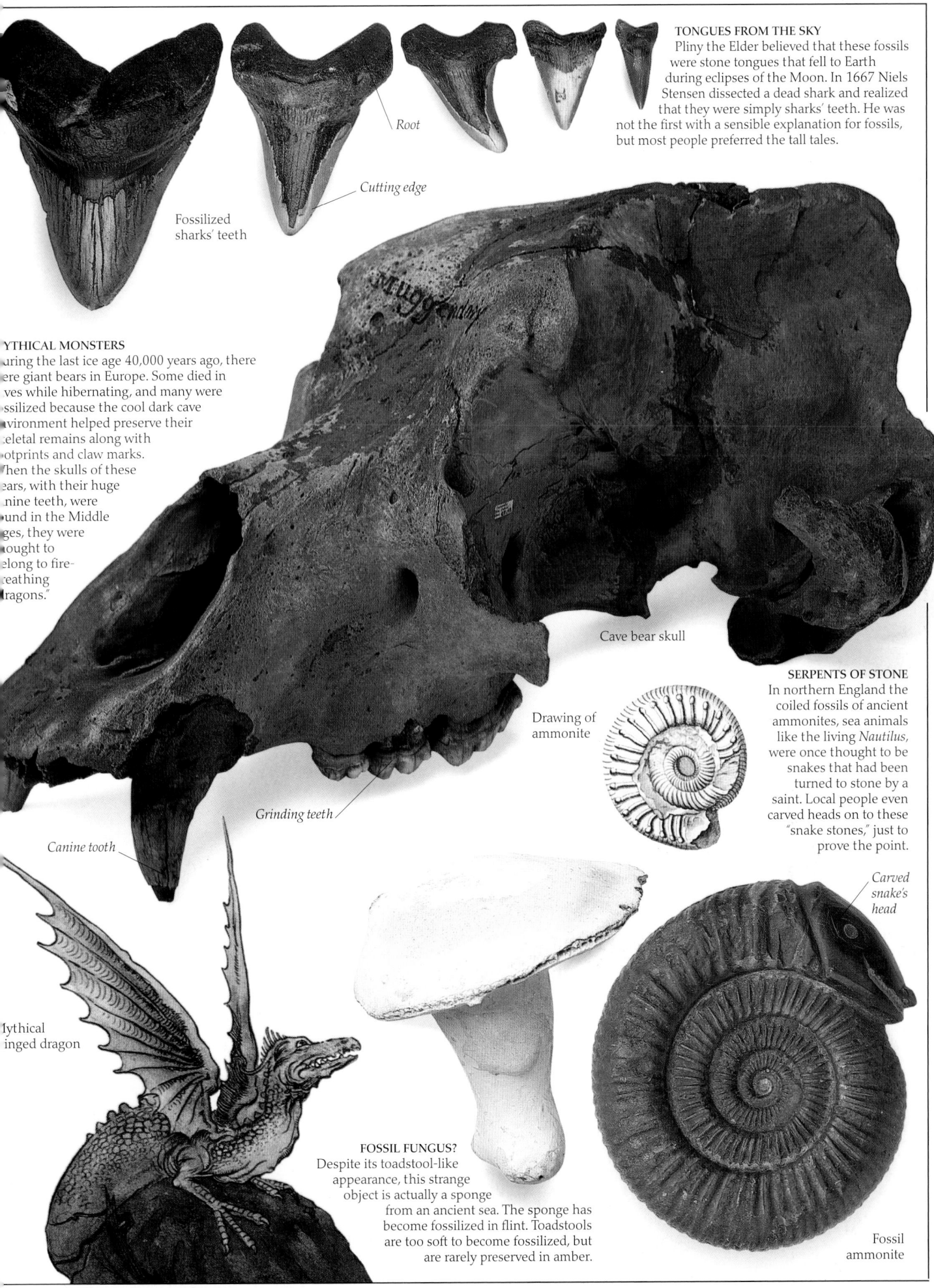

TONGUES FROM THE SKY
Pliny the Elder believed that these fossils were stone tongues that fell to Earth during eclipses of the Moon. In 1667 Niels Stensen dissected a dead shark and realized that they were simply sharks' teeth. He was not the first with a sensible explanation for fossils, but most people preferred the tall tales.

MYTHICAL MONSTERS
During the last ice age 40,000 years ago, there were giant bears in Europe. Some died in caves while hibernating, and many were fossilized because the cool dark cave environment helped preserve their skeletal remains along with footprints and claw marks. When the skulls of these bears, with their huge canine teeth, were found in the Middle Ages, they were thought to belong to fire-breathing dragons."

SERPENTS OF STONE
In northern England the coiled fossils of ancient ammonites, sea animals like the living *Nautilus*, were once thought to be snakes that had been turned to stone by a saint. Local people even carved heads on to these "snake stones," just to prove the point.

FOSSIL FUNGUS?
Despite its toadstool-like appearance, this strange object is actually a sponge from an ancient sea. The sponge has become fossilized in flint. Toadstools are too soft to become fossilized, but are rarely preserved in amber.

Victims of the flood

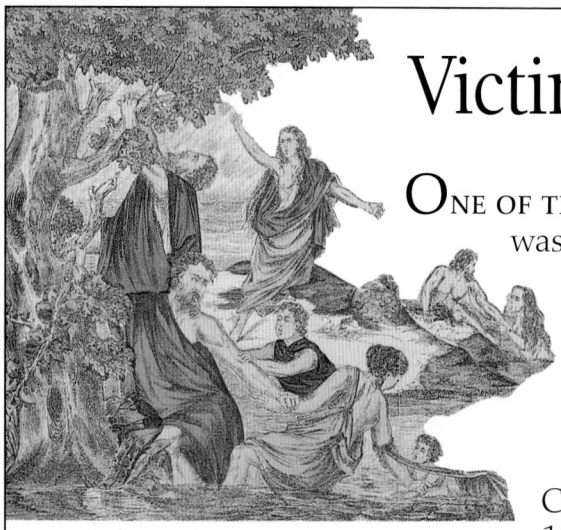

ONE OF THE GREATEST PUZZLES about fossils was the appearance of shells and other sea creatures high up on mountaintops. Some Ancient Greek scholars, such as Pythagoras and Herodotus, reasoned that such mountain rocks must once have been under the sea, but the early Christian philosopher Tertullian (around 155–222 CE) claimed that the waters of the flood, as described in the Bible, had carried shells up to this height. This idea was considered by Leonardo da Vinci (1452–1519), who made careful observations of fossils and calculated what would happen during a massive flood. He concluded that the explanation made no sense. Despite Leonardo's efforts, the idea was popular among geologists until the late 18th century. By then the theor was known as diluvialism. It proposed that all Earth's sedimentary rocks (made of sand, mud, and lime) had been deposited by floods when all the victims had been drowned and preserved as fossils within them. As a popular notion, rather than a scientific theory, it survived among fundamentalists into the 19th century, but by 1820 the evidence against it was so strong that the idea had largely disappeared.

NOAH AND THE FLOOD
The Bible describes an immense flood that covered all Earth's land and lasted for 40 days. Noah had been told by God to build an ark and take on board a male and a female of every kind of animal, so that none of them would die out completely. This part of the story led to great debates when the fossils of large extinct animals were discovered (pp. 14–15).

Shelly rock from the top of Mount Snowdon in Wales

FOSSIL HUNTER
Johann Scheuzer (1672–1733), a Swiss fossil collector, was an enthusiastic "diluvialist"—one who believed that the flood had created all sedimentary rocks and fossils. He described one of his finds as "the bony skeleton of one of those infamous men whose sins brought upon the world the dire misfortune of the deluge." It was a fossil of a giant salamander.

RAISING THE ROCKS
During the 18th and 19th centuries, geologists began to understand how sea shells could appear on mountaintops. They realized that most sedimentary rocks had been deposited in the sea as sand, mud, and lime. Here the remains of dead organisms were buried and fossilized as the sediment turned to rock. Later Earth movements squeezed and broke the rocks, buckling them into folds, so that rocks that had been under the sea were raised into mountains.

he missing fossils

ll fossils were creatures killed by flood, there would be fossils of at many land animals that were wned as the waters rose, but few sils of fish, since they could swim. fact, the opposite is true. Seafloor atures are some of the most mmon fossils, while land animals relatively rare. However, land vironments such as swamps d lakes, and their life are metimes fossilized.

Rare fossil of an insect

Uncommon dragonfly fossil

Lizard

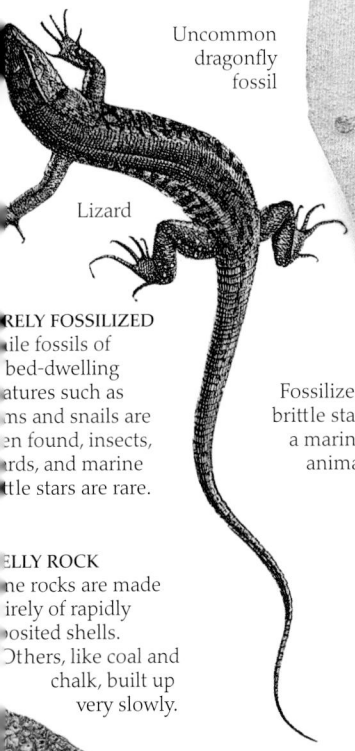

RELY FOSSILIZED
ile fossils of bed-dwelling atures such as ms and snails are en found, insects, rds, and marine ttle stars are rare.

ELLY ROCK
ne rocks are made irely of rapidly osited shells. Others, like coal and chalk, built up very slowly.

Fossilized brittle star, a marine animal

Fossil perch

Chalk and coal

As people learned more about sedimentary rocks, it became clear that these cannot all have been laid down in a few years. Chalk and coal, for example, are made up of the remains of living things—trillions of microscopic shells, in the case of chalk, and thousands of plant remains piled one upon another for coal. Clearly, such rocks must have taken a very long time to build up.

ROCK OF AGES
In 1858 a geologist, looking at chalk under the microscope, found that it was almost entirely made up of tiny shells. These shells belonged to microscopic creatures that floated at the ocean's surface. We know this because their relatives still do so today. Chalk cliffs (above) show how thick the layers of chalk are.

MICROSCOPIC STRUCTURE
When chalk is imaged under an electron microscope, its structure reveals that it is made up almost entirely of the calcareous (calcium-rich) skeletons of minute creatures.

Fern fossil in coal

THE COAL FORESTS
Coal is made almost entirely of plant remains from bogs and swampy forests. When the plants died, their tissues did not rot away but gradually turned into peat. This was then compressed by the growing weight above it, turning it into coal. Coal seams can be 65 ft (20 m) thick.

Jean-Baptiste de Lamarck

REVOLUTIONARY THINKER
French naturalist Lamarck made people think about evolution.

JEAN-BAPTISTE DE LAMARCK (1744–1829) was one of the first people propose a theory of evolution. He believed that there were two evolutionary forces at work. The first was a "tendency to progression," a automatic process by which all living things became more complex. Th second force was the need to fit in with the local environment: as animals tried to fit in, their efforts produced a bodily change. In this wa the giraffe developed a long neck by stretching for the leaves of trees, and wading birds grew long legs by straining upward to keep themselv dry. These two forces were not in harmony, according to Lamarck. The first force working alone would produce perfect patterns of increasing complexity among animals, but the second force interfered with the first. For the second force to work, characteristics acquired by the parents (such as a longer neck) would have to be passed on to their offspring. This is now known not to happen, except in a few rare cases, but in Lamarck's day it was a common idea. For a century afterward, everyone, including Darwin (p. 20), believed it to be true. Today, the term "Lamarckism" is often used just to mean the inheritance of acquired characteristics. The other parts of Lamarck's theory have largely been forgotten.

HIGH AND D
According to Lamarck's theory, trying to keep its belly out of t water a wading bird "acquires t habit of stretching and elongati its legs." In this way, he believe species such as this purple her developed their long le

Subtle fluids

Lamarck suggested that there were "subtle fluids" flowing all around a body and all through it, and that these produced both movement and change. He regarded the fluids as mysterious, but believed he could identify two: caloric (heat) and electricity.

CHARGED IDEAS
Lamarck believed that his "subtle fluids" were involved in both kinds of change—the "tendency to progression" and the striving to fit local conditions. Electricity was of great interest to scientists at the time, and it appealed to Lamarck because it could be felt but not seen. The French scientist Jean-Antoine Nollet (1700–1770) set up experiments (right) to study the effects of static electricity on plants and animals.

FEELING THE WAY FORWARD
Lamarck used snails as an examp of how "subtle fluids" worked. Snails have poor vision, and he imagined an ancestral snail with no feelers, groping around with i head. Its efforts to feel the way would send "masses of nervous fluid as well as other liquids" to the front of the head. In time this would produce "eye-tipped tentacles."

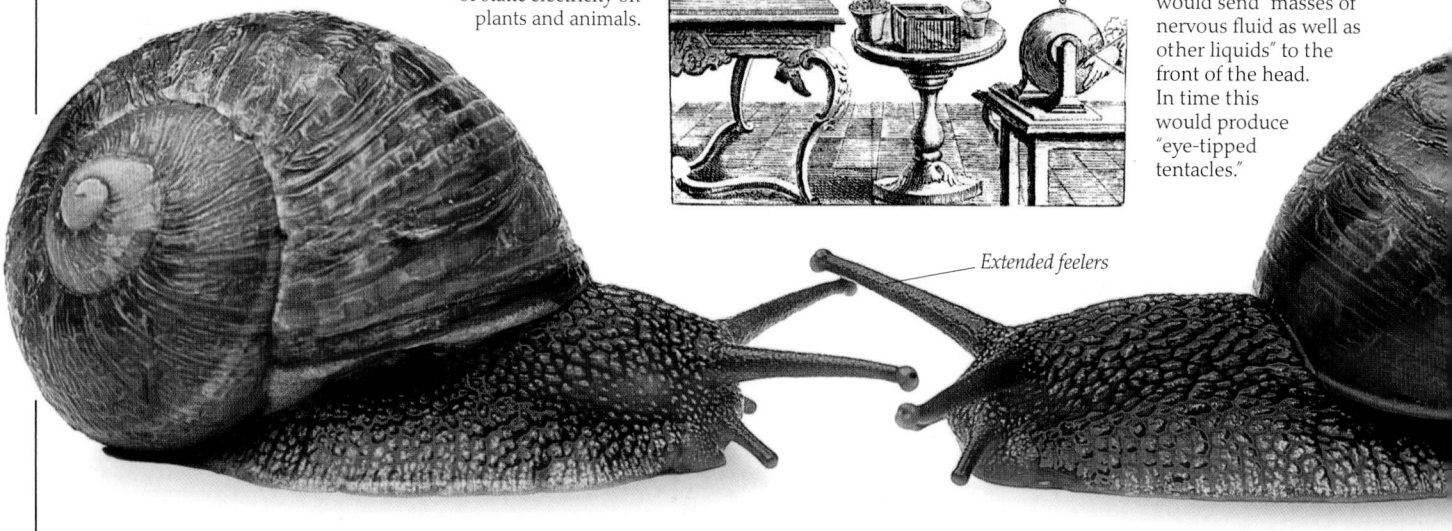

ooking at the evidence

support his claim that evolution had urred, Lamarck pointed to the way t members of a species, such as a terfly species, can vary from place to ce. His ideas about the inheritance of uired characteristics and about the ntinuous creation of simple life forms re later proven to be false.

Agrias claudina claudina
Eastern Central Brazil

Agrias claudina claudianus
Southeastern Brazil

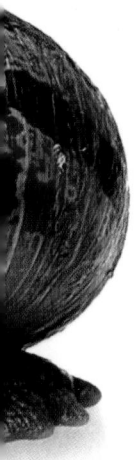

Agrias claudina sardanapalus
Peru and Brazil

Agrias claudina lugens
Peru

Agrias claudina godmani
Central Brazil

Agrias claudina intermedius
Southeastern Colombia, Venezuela

MAKING NEW SPECIES
These lovely butterflies from different areas of South America illustrate Lamarck's point about variation within a species. Those from different areas can all interbreed, so they must all belong to the same species. They are called "subspecies." Lamarck also observed that closely related species (p. 22) can look very much alike, as similar as these subspecies. From this he concluded that related species had developed from a set of subspecies. This idea is now thought to be correct, although exactly how new species are formed is still being debated (p. 40).

SPONTANEOUS LIFE
If all living things are progressing, why are there still simple creatures left? Lamarck believed that new ones arose by "spontaneous generation" of microscopic life from nonliving matter, such as wet straw. French microbiologist Louis Pasteur (1822–1895) showed this to be an illusion. If the straw was boiled thoroughly, no living things developed.

PASSING IT ON
If acquired characteristics were inherited, as Lamarck thought, then the children of white-skinned people living in hot countries would be born with sun-tanned skins. This English family in 19th-century India shows that they are not.

POET AND BOTANIST
Even before Lamarck, the poet Johann Goethe (1749–1832) had published evolutionary ideas about plants.

Extinct animals

SCIENTIFIC PRESIDENT
US President Thomas Jefferson (1743–1826) was also a fossil collector. At first he could not accept that any animal had become extinct, but in time the evidence of the fossil finds convinced him that they had.

According to the Bible, Noah took two of every kind of animal into his ark, and all survived the Flood. Christianity also taught that each living thing was an essential link in God's chain of creation. Thus, it would be impossible for any of them to have died out completely, or become "extinct." When fossils of unknown creatures were found, it was assumed that the animals were still living somewhere in the world. However, by the end of the 18th century, the fossils of such gigantic creatures had been found that this explanation began to seem unlikely. In North America the massive bones of the giant ground sloth and the mastodon were discovered. No unexplored regions were large enough to hide such giants, and the suspicion that they had become extinct began to grow. French scientists, less influenced by religious views following the upheavals of the French Revolution, were among the first to accept the idea of extinction. Afterward, the idea was accepted in the US, and then, more slowly, in other countries.

LOST WORLDS
The strange duck-billed platypus of Australia was only discovered by western science in 1799. Discoveries like this suggested that there were many unknown creatures in the world and that "extinct" animals could still be alive somewhere.

HARD TO HIDE
This is a cross-section, shown half life-size, through the upper molar teeth of a giant ground sloth, known as *Megatherium*. The fossils of another ground sloth, almost as large, were found in North America and first described by Thomas Jefferson in 1797. A living animal of this size could clearly not remain undiscovered, unlike small animals such as the platypus. By the 1830s the idea of extinction had become widely accepted.

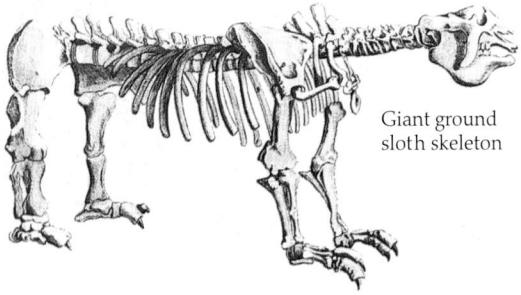

Giant ground sloth skeleton

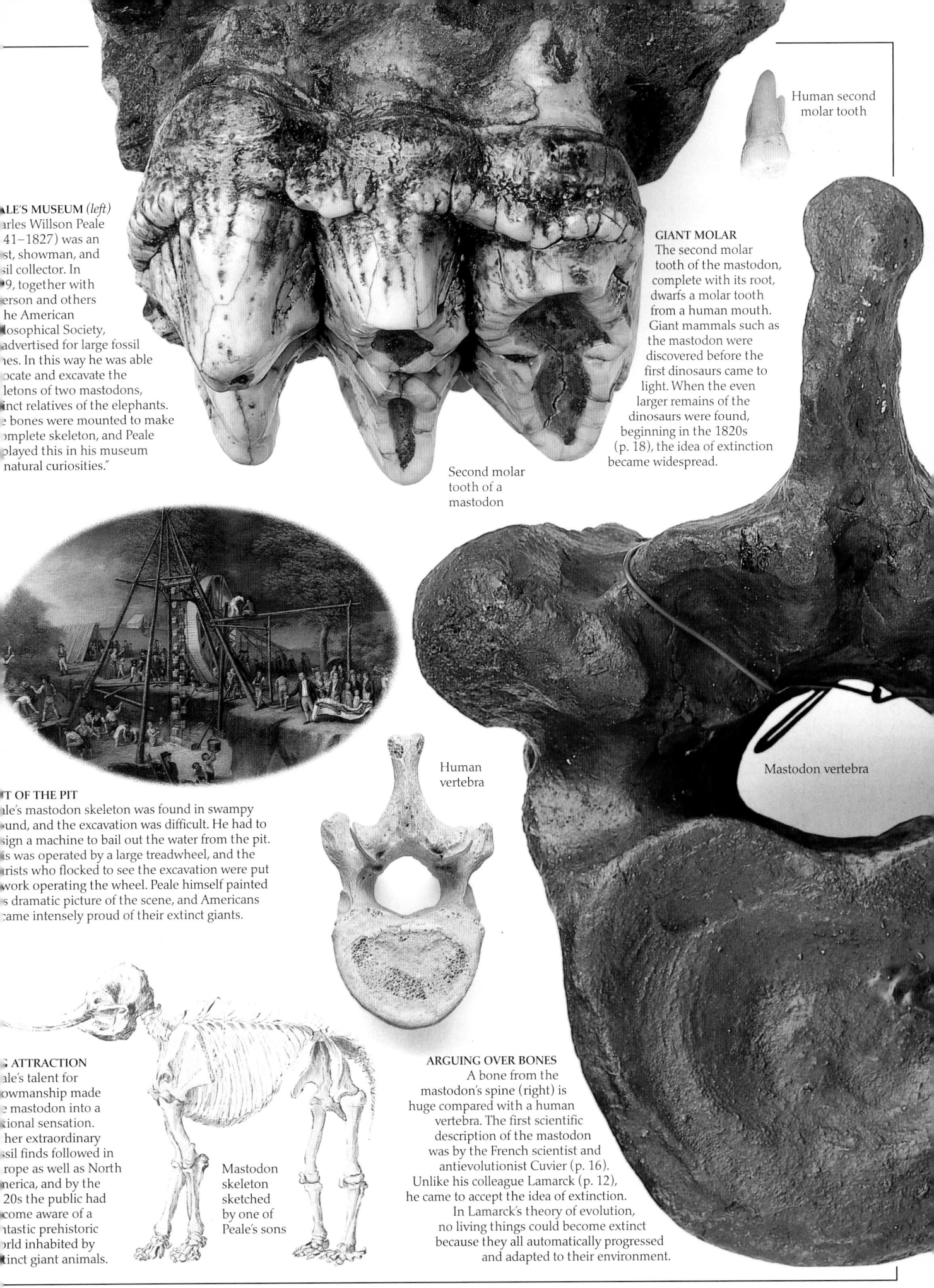

LE'S MUSEUM *(left)*
arles Willson Peale
41–1827) was an
st, showman, and
sil collector. In
9, together with
erson and others
he American
osophical Society,
advertised for large fossil
nes. In this way he was able
ocate and excavate the
letons of two mastodons,
inct relatives of the elephants.
bones were mounted to make
omplete skeleton, and Peale
played this in his museum
natural curiosities."

GIANT MOLAR
The second molar tooth of the mastodon, complete with its root, dwarfs a molar tooth from a human mouth. Giant mammals such as the mastodon were discovered before the first dinosaurs came to light. When the even larger remains of the dinosaurs were found, beginning in the 1820s (p. 18), the idea of extinction became widespread.

T OF THE PIT
ale's mastodon skeleton was found in swampy
und, and the excavation was difficult. He had to
sign a machine to bail out the water from the pit.
is was operated by a large treadwheel, and the
rists who flocked to see the excavation were put
work operating the wheel. Peale himself painted
s dramatic picture of the scene, and Americans
came intensely proud of their extinct giants.

ATTRACTION
ale's talent for
owmanship made
mastodon into a
ional sensation.
her extraordinary
sil finds followed in
rope as well as North
nerica, and by the
20s the public had
come aware of a
ntastic prehistoric
orld inhabited by
tinct giant animals.

Mastodon skeleton sketched by one of Peale's sons

ARGUING OVER BONES
A bone from the mastodon's spine (right) is huge compared with a human vertebra. The first scientific description of the mastodon was by the French scientist and antievolutionist Cuvier (p. 16). Unlike his colleague Lamarck (p. 12), he came to accept the idea of extinction.
In Lamarck's theory of evolution, no living things could become extinct because they all automatically progressed and adapted to their environment.

A series of catastrophes

GEORGES CUVIER
Cuvier believed that catastrophes had stripped much of Earth of life several times, but that some regions had always escaped, and animals had spread again from those regions. Later he also accepted that some animals had become extinct, while Lamarck refused to believe this. Cuvier was against evolution, believing that life had "stood still" between catastrophes. Lamarck and Cuvier became life-long enemies.

INDUSTRIAL EXPANSION in the 18th century created a need for iron ore and coal, as well as canals for transportation. Mines and excavations went deep underground, which led to great advances in geology. By the late 18th century the German naturalist Abraham Werner (1750–1817) had divided rock strata into three groups—Primary, Secondary, and Tertiary, from oldest to youngest. Werner thought that all these strata had been laid down by a series of catastrophic worldwide floods. By the beginning of the 19th century, it was realized independently by William Smith (1769–1839) in England and Georges Cuvier (1769–1832) in France that fossils coul be used to characterize successive strata. Cuvier also thought that successive strat resulted from a series of catastrophic floods. Nevertheless, fossils were shown to be particularly useful for subdividing rock strata and mapping their distribution for the first time. By the mid-19th century, geologists such as Charles Lyell (1797–1875) were arguing that sedimentary rock strata were not laid down by catastrophic events but rather by everyday, gradual processes of erosion and depostion. The subdivision of geological strata and time was refined by many European geologists into a series of geological periods such as the Carboniferous and Jurassic (p. 28).

UNCHANGED IBIS
The modern ibis is indeed the same as that of ancient Egypt Some species do stay much same for thousands, or eve millions, of years, while other species can evolve very rapidly. It all depen on the circumstances. Lamarck and Cuvier we each right on one poin and wrong on another. Lamarck was right in thinking that species were not fixed, but Cuvier was partly right about mass extinctions (p. 46).

EVIDENCE FROM EGYPT
Napoleon's troops invaded Egypt in 1798 and brought back mummies found in the pyramids. Among these was a mummified ibis, and Cuvier was jubilant to find that its skeleton was the same as that of a living ibis. He claimed this absence of change as evidence that Lamarck was wrong and that evolution did not occur.

Egyptian sculpture of an ibis

Modern ibis

Mummified ibis

iam Smith

CLUES FROM CANALS
From childhood William Smith collected fossils, and later developed a professional interest in rocks and fossils while working as an engineer and surveyor on the construction of canals. He found that successive strata could be characterized by their fossils and always occur in the same sequence. This allowed him to identify and map the succession of strata across the landscape matching otherwise separate outcrops from one part of the country to another.

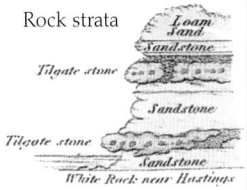

Rock strata

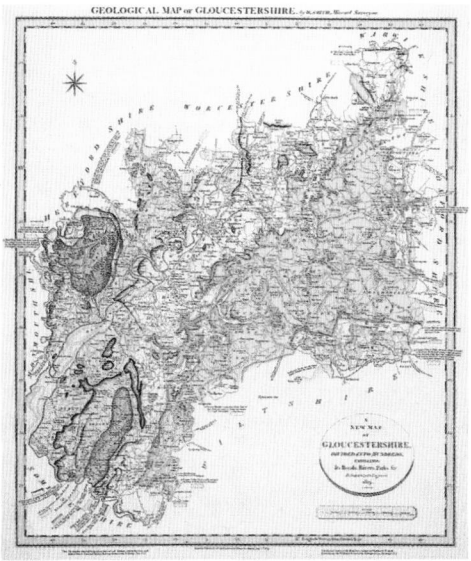

One of Smith's geological maps showing strata as different colors

Fossil fish found by Miller

ER'S FISH
h Miller
2–1856), a deeply
ious man, found fossils
tinct armored fish. He
ved, wrongly, that they were
advanced than living fish and
them as part of an earlier creation
oyed by a catastrophe. Miller's
s, trying to reconcile geology
the Bible, were
popular.

Hugh Miller, Scottish stone mason and fossil hunter

CONTROVERSIAL FINDS
Miller helped to popularize a new religious version of catastrophe theory. It held that there had been several successive creations, each destroyed by a catastrophe, and that the Bible told only of the last creation. All fossils of extinct animals were from earlier creations. This theory was dealt a blow by finds from several British caves of extinct animals alongside handmade stone tools.

Miller's paper model of extinct fish

THE ICE MAN
American scientist Louis Agassiz (1807–1873), a follower of Cuvier, added a new type of catastrophe—the Ice Ages. Agassiz's theories were initially rejected by many uniformitarians, such as Charles Lyell (1797–1875), who believed that all geological change was gradual. Modern geology has shown that both processes are at work. There are gradual and generally predictable processes. Then there are less predictable events on different scales, such as catastrophic earthquakes, storms, tsunamis, extra-terrestrial impacts, ice ages, and rapid climate change.

Hand ax made by early people

Mammoth tooth found with hand ax

Dinosaur frenzy

DIGGING FOR *IGUANODON*
Excavations at the quarry in Sussex, southern England, from which Gideon Mantell's *Iguanodon* teeth originally came.

FOSSILIZED DINOSAUR BONES were discovered as early as the 17th century, but they were not recognized as giant reptiles. The breakthrough came with Gideon Mantell (1804–1892), a British doctor and fossil hunter. In 1822 he found some large and unusual teeth that he showed to Cuvier (p. 16) and William Buckland, a British geologist. Both dismissed them as unimportant, but Mantell was convinced they were wrong and continued his research. Eventually he found that the teeth resembled those of iguana lizards. Calling his find *Iguanodon* (iguana-tooth), he published a description of a lizard 40 ft (12 m) long. In the meantime, Buckland had found his own giant reptile. Such finds continued, but the name dinosaur ("terrible lizard") was not used until 1841, when it was coined by Richard Owen, a celebrated anatomist and follower of Cuvier. Dinosaurs created a sensation because they were so spectacularly different from anything still alive. They remained headline news throughout the 19th century, making everyone aware of the distant past and its strange animals. This awareness set the stage for evolutionary ideas. Yet Owen used the dinosaurs as an argument against evolution, claiming that they were more advanced than living reptiles. Modern evolution theory recognizes that evolution does not always mean progress (p. 48). If the environment changes, more advanced animals can die out while their less advanced relatives survive.

SURPRISING FINDS
William Buckland (1784–1856) displays some prize specimens. The long-beaked skull at the front is an ichthyosaur, a marine reptile that belonged to a separate group from the dinosau The first ichthyosaur was described in 1810 bu was thought to be a crocodile. In 1824 Bucklan found jaw fragments and other bones of a dinosaur called *Megalosaurus*. Richard Owen supervised the making of a model *Megalosauru* (below) in the 1850s, before any complete dinosaur skeletons had been found. With so lit evidence Owen made a good guess, but the model is largely wrong. The same sculptor made the *Iguanodon* model opposite.

CONTROVERSIAL MODELS
This model of *Megalosaurus*, based on fossils described by Buckland, was later made into a life-size dinosaur and put on show at the Crystal Palace in London alongside others. When the city fathers of New York commissioned a similar exhibition for Central Park, a local judge attacked the models as "antireligious," and the plan ended when someone broke into the workshop and destroyed all the models.

Jaw fragments found by Buckland

Fragments fitted into outline of skull

DARWIN'S ENEMY
Richard Owen (1804–1892), who coined the word "dinosaur," also wrote a scathing review of Darwin's *The Origin of Species* and predicted that Darwin would be forgotten in 10 years' time. In later life, Owen resented Darwin's fame and implied that he had developed an evolutionary theory of his own long before Darwin. Owen was present when, on New Year's Eve, 1853, 21 scientists ate dinner inside his model of the *Iguanodon* (below) before it joined other dinosaur models at London's Crystal Palace.

GIDEON MANTELL
On the basis of the bones and teeth that he had found, Mantell imagined *Iguanodon* to be like a large lizard. In his reconstruction Mantell placed the hornlike spike (below) on the tip of the animal's nose. It was later discovered to be a thumb spike.

DOZENS OF DINOSAURS
In 1878 coal miners in Belgium found 39 *Iguanodon* skeletons. Fossil footprints suggested that *Iguanodon* might have walked on its hind legs. It was believed to have stood semi-upright, so the skeletons of an emu and a wallaby were studied for this Belgian reconstruction.

Cast of *Iguanodon* "horn"

Misplaced umb spike

CHANGING IDEAS
This modern view of *Iguanodon* is based on detailed studies of marks on the bones, which can reveal much about muscles and tendons. They show that it walked mainly on two legs, with its horizontal body balanced by a rigid tail.

SCALING UP
This model *Iguanodon* and other models were later scaled up to make the giant reptiles displayed at the Crystal Palace since 1854.

CRET AUTHOR
1844, as dinosaur discoveries azed the public, a pro-evolution ok called *The Vestiges of Creation* s published. Robert Chambers 02–1871) was revealed as its hor only after his death. Chambers d to make evolution pectable but was heavily icized by scientists for ccuracies. Even it was very pular and ned Darwin potential blems.

Charles Darwin

CHARLES DARWIN (1809–1882), THE ENGLISH NATURALIST, is well known as the author of *The Origin of Species*. He was not the first to think of evolution, and his real achievement was to present a coherent argument for evolution backed up by a mass of accurate information. In the early 19th century the concept of evolution was very unpopular. Lamarck's theory (p. 12) had been taken up in revolutionary France in the 1790s because it challenged the authority of the church and the king. The fear of a similar revolution in England made evolution a scandalous idea. In fact, the zoologist Professor Robert Grant lost his position at the University of London and died in poverty because he openly supported Lamarck's views. When an anonymous book on evolution, *The Vestiges of Creation* (p. 19), was published in 1844, it met with outrage. All this encouraged Darwin to keep quiet for as long as possible. "It is like confessing a murder," he wrote to a friend as his theory steadily took shape in his mind. In 1858, when the naturalist Alfred Wallace also hit upon the idea of natural selection (p. 36), Darwin was finally forced to publish.

Telescope us on the *Beagl*

Darwin's compass

TAKING NOTES
While living aboard the *Beagle*, Darwin took up the habit of making careful observations of the natural world. He also made long and detailed notes, recording everything that he saw, and he thought hard about the meaning of his scientific observations.

One of Darwin's notebooks

Charles Darwin

HMS *Beagle*

From 1832 to 1836 Darwin was invited on the *Beagle*'s world voyage by Captain Fitzroy as companion and naturalist. In South America, and particularly in the Galapagos Islands, he noted many puzzling features of the plants and animals that lived there. He later understood that these peculiarities were the results of evolution.

THINKING AFLOAT
Darwin was not an evolutionist when he stepped aboard HMS *Beagle*, nor when he returned. But over the next five years the idea took shape in his mind. He was never dogmatic about his theory but considered all his opponents' views carefully. In later years this approach helped Darwin to gain support from some of the leading naturalists of his day—even those who had previously rejected evolution.

GOING ASHORE
On the voyage, Darwin took with him a copy of Charles Lyell's new book *Principles of Geology* in which Lyell claimed that the geological features of Earth could be explained by slow-acting forces that were still at work, such as the laying down of sediment. Darwin spent much time ashore, and his observations of geology confirmed Lyell's theory, implying that Earth was very old.

People of Tierra del Fuego greet the *Beagle*

A great naturalist

Before the *Beagle* voyage, Darwin studied to be a clergyman at Cambridge University. While there, he developed a passionate interest in natural history—an interest that was to change the course of his life.

ERASMUS DARWIN
Charles's grandfather, Erasmus Darwin (1731–1802), was a doctor, poet, and botanist. He was also a friend of scientists and industrialists, such as Joseph Priestley and Josiah Wedgwood, who questioned conventional ideas and were considered dangerous. Even before Lamarck (p. 12) he wrote a long epic poem about evolution. The next generation of the Darwin family, anxious to seem more respectable, largely ignored Erasmus's books.

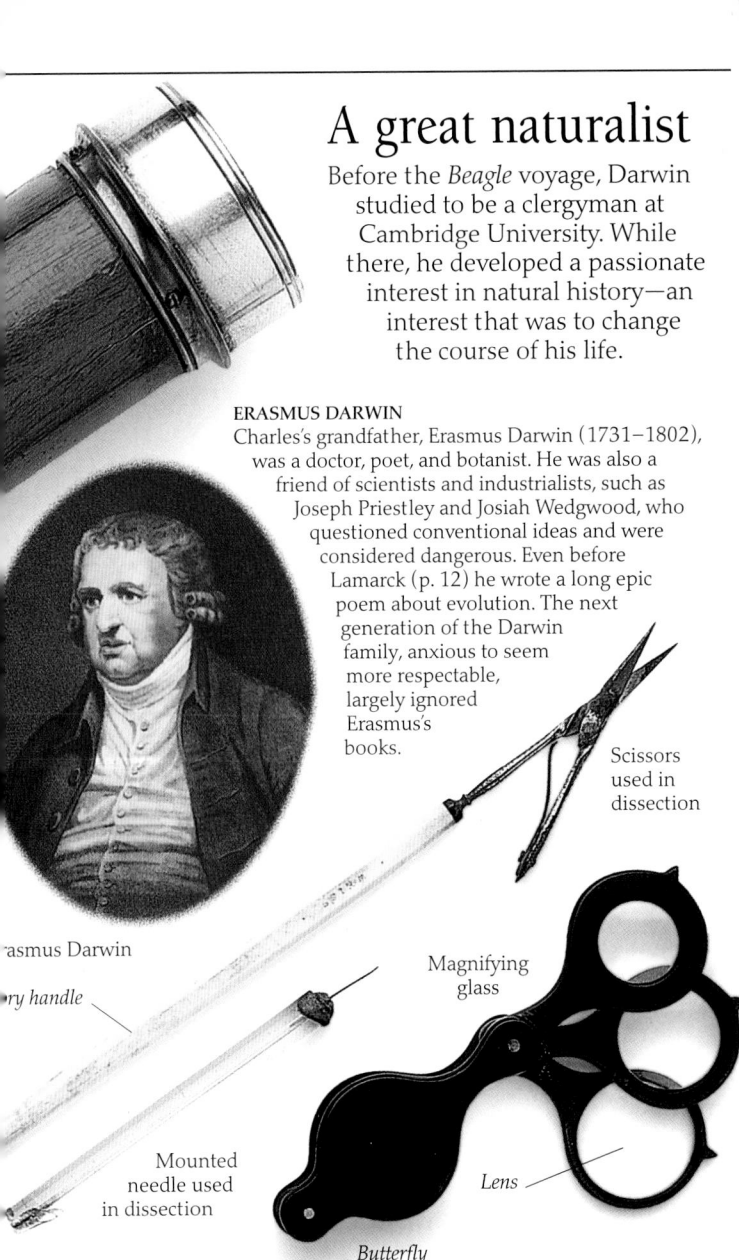

Part of Darwin's beetle collection

BEETLE MANIA
During his student days at Cambridge, Darwin was an enthusiastic collector of beetles. This is part of his enormous collection. Being an experienced practical naturalist was a great strength for Darwin. When it came to discussing plants and animals, he had firsthand knowledge of the subject.

ALL ABOUT WORMS
After writing *The Origin of Species*, Darwin continued his work as a naturalist. He felt that looking at the small details of living things was just as important as devising grand theories. One of his later books was devoted entirely to earthworms, which clearly puzzled this cartoonist.

A cartoon from the humorous magazine *Punch*

llecting boxes, beetle, d microscope slide m Down House

COLLECTING DATA
Darwin grew many plants in the greenhouses at his home, Down House. He was particularly interested in climbing and twining plants, insect-eating plants, and orchids. He dissected the flowers of orchids and made some amazing discoveries about how these flowers are pollinated. Other naturalists sent him seeds or whole plants that might interest him, and some of the seed packets have survived to this day (right). Darwin's work would have made him famous as a great biologist even if he had never written *The Origin of Species*.

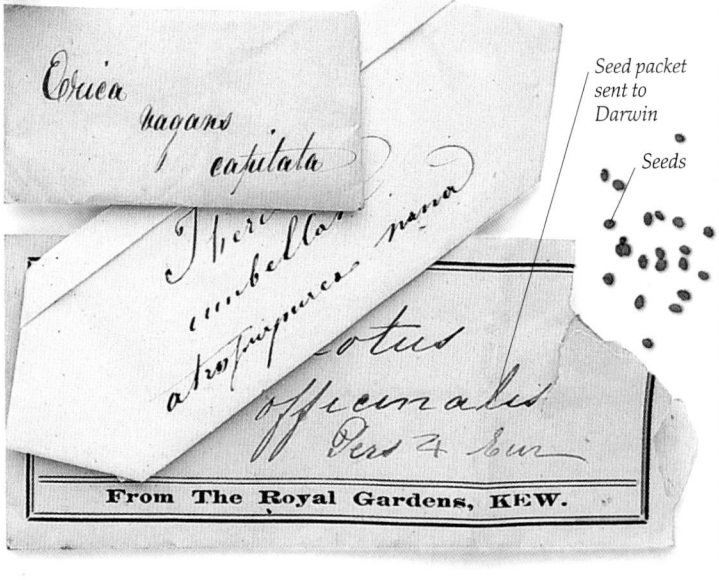

Seed packet sent to Darwin

Seeds

Living evidence

THINKING THE SAME WAY
Constantine Rafinesque was an eccentric American naturalist who saw the signs of evolution.

DARWIN SET HIMSELF two major tasks. One was to work out a mechanism by which evolution might occur. The mechanism he thought of was natural selection (p. 36), which is still accepted today as the main force behind evolution. His other task was to collect enough evidence to convince people that evolution had occurred. Some evidence came from fossils (p. 26) or from plant and animal distribution (p. 24). Most important was the evidence from living things. This was clear enough to have been noticed by other naturalists, including Rafinesque, who wrote in 1836, "All species might have been varieties once, and many varieties are gradually becoming species." Such casual remarks by naturalists carried little weight, but Darwin was more difficult to ignore because he produced so much data. One important piece of evidence was that the same basic pattern of bones appears in the limbs of all mammals. Such similarities show that they must all be descended from a common ancestor.

CHIMPANZEE'S ARM
The arm and hand of t chimpanzee are close t the basic vertebrate pattern, having five fingers, five hand bone a set of small bones in the wrist, two lower ar bones, and one upper arm bone. In these drawings the different bones are color-coded.

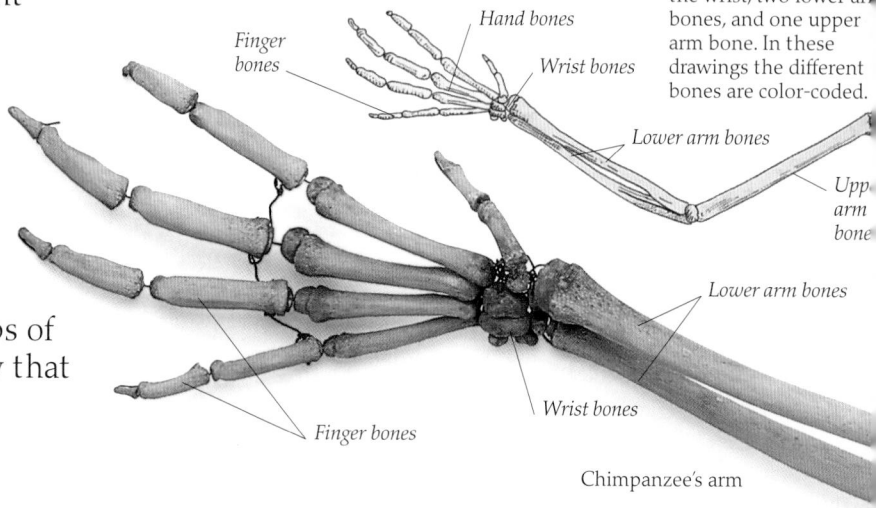

Chimpanzee's arm

BEE ORCHIDS
These Mediterranean bee orchids look remarkably similar, but they cannot interbreed. Therefore, each of them belongs to a separate species. Each species is pollinated by a different type of insect, and this acts as an isolating mechanism (p. 41). Darwin and Rafinesque were both struck by groups of very similar species such as these. It seemed obvious that they must have evolved from a single ancestral species. This ancestor probably developed into a number of varieties or subspecies (p. 13) first.

Bat

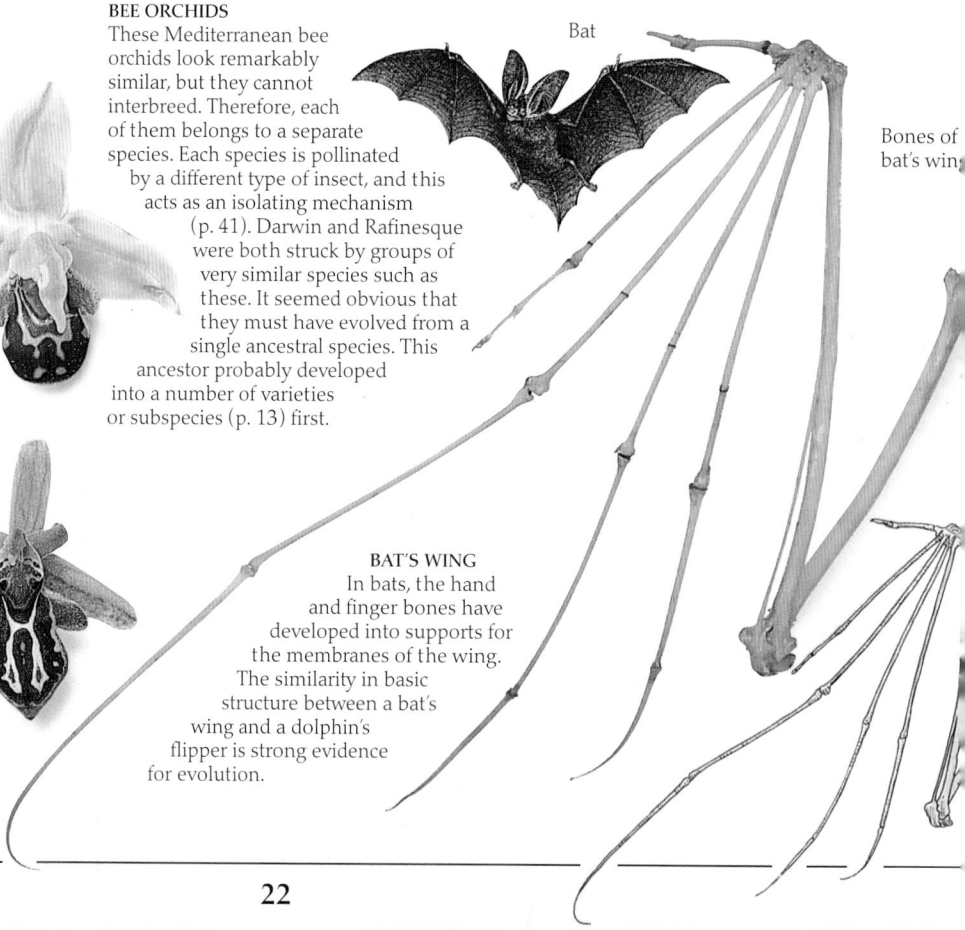

Bones of bat's win

BAT'S WING
In bats, the hand and finger bones have developed into supports for the membranes of the wing. The similarity in basic structure between a bat's wing and a dolphin's flipper is strong evidence for evolution.

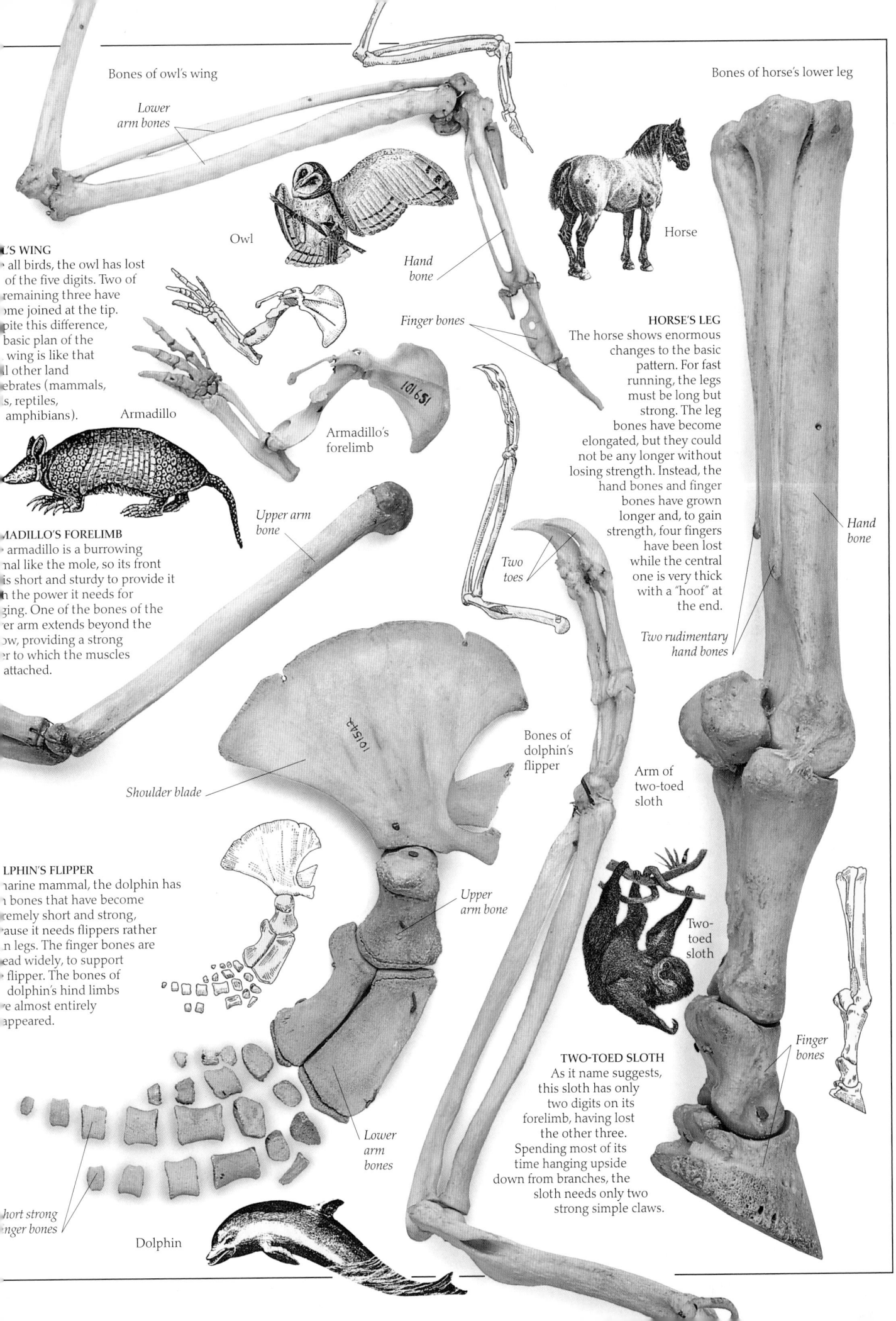

L'S WING
• all birds, the owl has lost of the five digits. Two of remaining three have ome joined at the tip. pite this difference, basic plan of the wing is like that ll other land ebrates (mammals, s, reptiles, amphibians).

MADILLO'S FORELIMB
• armadillo is a burrowing nal like the mole, so its front is short and sturdy to provide it h the power it needs for ging. One of the bones of the er arm extends beyond the ow, providing a strong r to which the muscles attached.

LPHIN'S FLIPPER
narine mammal, the dolphin has n bones that have become remely short and strong, ause it needs flippers rather n legs. The finger bones are ead widely, to support flipper. The bones of dolphin's hind limbs e almost entirely appeared.

HORSE'S LEG
The horse shows enormous changes to the basic pattern. For fast running, the legs must be long but strong. The leg bones have become elongated, but they could not be any longer without losing strength. Instead, the hand bones and finger bones have grown longer and, to gain strength, four fingers have been lost while the central one is very thick with a "hoof" at the end.

TWO-TOED SLOTH
As it name suggests, this sloth has only two digits on its forelimb, having lost the other three. Spending most of its time hanging upside down from branches, the sloth needs only two strong simple claws.

hort strong nger bones

Animal and plant distribution

PLANT HUNTER
The botanist Joseph Hooker (1817–1911) searched for new plants in the Himalayas and New Zealand and was director of the Royal Botanic Gardens at Kew, near London. Darwin's good friend and colleague, he told him a great deal about plant distribution.

IN DARWIN'S TIME, it was believed that each species had been created by God to suit best the conditions of a particular place. This "special creation" theory had many weak points, as Darwin made clear. In Australia mammals introduced from Europe had overrun the country, wiping out some native mammals. If Australian animals were exactly right for Australia, how could this happen? Darwin showed how migration and evolution could explain the patterns of distribution far better. Islands were an important part of his argument. The animals of the Cape Verde Islands are basically like those in Africa, and the Galapagos animals are like South American animals. Since these two island groups have much the same conditions, why had the Creator not made similar animals for them? Darwin suggested that animals and plants had arrived from the nearest mainland. Some had then evolved into unique types.

Thick bony plate from the outer cove of a Glyptodon

ARMORED ANCESTOR
While in South America, Darwin found the remains of a *Glyptodon*, a prehistoric giant armored mammal. He realized that it resembled the livin armadillos of South America. This continuity between animals of the past and present had als been found in Australia, and it provided strong supporting evidence for the idea of evolution.

Fossilized skull of *Glyptodon*

Illustration of *Glyptodon*

ONCE ON AN ISLAND
The modern armadillo is just one of the many unusual mammals of South America. If animals and plants could travel freely, there should be roughly the same species everywhere, but, in fact, there are many blocks to migration, such as oceans, deserts, and mountain ranges. South America was an island for millions of years, and many unique mammals evolved there during this time.

Modern armadillo

ried mud

uck's
ot

edlings
rout from
d

New Zealand

The animals on these islands are well explained by evolution. Strong sea currents prevented most mammals from getting there, so birds and insects, which arrived by air, evolved to fill some of the slots normally taken by mammal species.

New Zealand

MOAS AND KIWIS
The flightless kiwi is found only in New Zealand, as were the giant flightless birds called moas, which are now extinct. Moas and kiwis evolved from flying birds that colonized the islands of New Zealand millions of years ago.

Kiwi

Giant moa

GIANT CRICKET
Because there are no mice in New Zealand, the giant bush cricket, or weta, has evolved to fill the slot that mice occupy elsewhere. In general, mammals are less able to cross oceans than are birds, reptiles or insects.

Weta, life size

GHOSTLY FOOT
The moas died out very recently because of overhunting. Their undecayed remains (not fossils) are still sometimes found in caves. This is a foot from this enormous bird.

ANDERING PLANTS
ow could plants travel to an island? This question was crucial Darwin. He imagined that waterbirds, which fly long distances d rest on islands, might unintentionally transport plant seeds. scraped dry mud from birds' feet and mixed it with water—edlings sprang up, as he had expected.

The Galapagos

is visit to the Galapagos islands provided Darwin ith some excellent evidence. In general, the imals of the islands resembled those of outh America, but many species were nique to the Galapagos.

Map of Galapagos Islands from *A Naturalist's Voyage Round the World* by Darwin

Galapagos finches

DARWIN'S FINCHES
The Galapagos finches are clearly related to a type of finch from South America. Each of the 13 species has a differently shaped beak. The beaks are adapted to different kinds of food ranging from insects to seeds.

ATTACKED BY BIRDS
Henry Bates (1825–1892) helped Darwin by supplying him with data on animals and plants in the Amazon rain forest. Bates was one of many naturalists to study distant parts of the world for the first time, and Darwin sought information from several of them.

IANCE LANDING
e Galapagos Islands are some 800 miles ,300 km) from South America. All the Galapagos ches are probably descended from a small ainland flock that was blown off course and ached the islands millions of years ago.

Fossil evidence

INSIDE STORY
Sliced in half, an ammonite reveals its intricate chambers.

DARWIN STUDIED the fossil record carefully for evidence that evolution had occurred. At the time fossils did not provide him with the evidence that he needed. He hoped that fossils would bridge the evolutionary gaps between the major groups of living animals but these were not immediately forthcoming. Darwin explained their absence by arguing that the rock record was far from complete. He was also aware that many paleontologists would use their expertise to criticize his evolutionary theory and so did not try to use fossils to support his theory. Today, we know that while the rock record does, in fact, have many gaps, there is now plenty of fossil evidence that fills the evolutionary gaps. For instance, the gradual evolution of the mammals from synapsid tetrapods is represented by a series of extinct fossils, such as the therapsid cynodonts. Darwin was also particularly concerned with the seemingly sudden appearance of life on Earth at the beginning of Cambrian times, 542 million years ago.

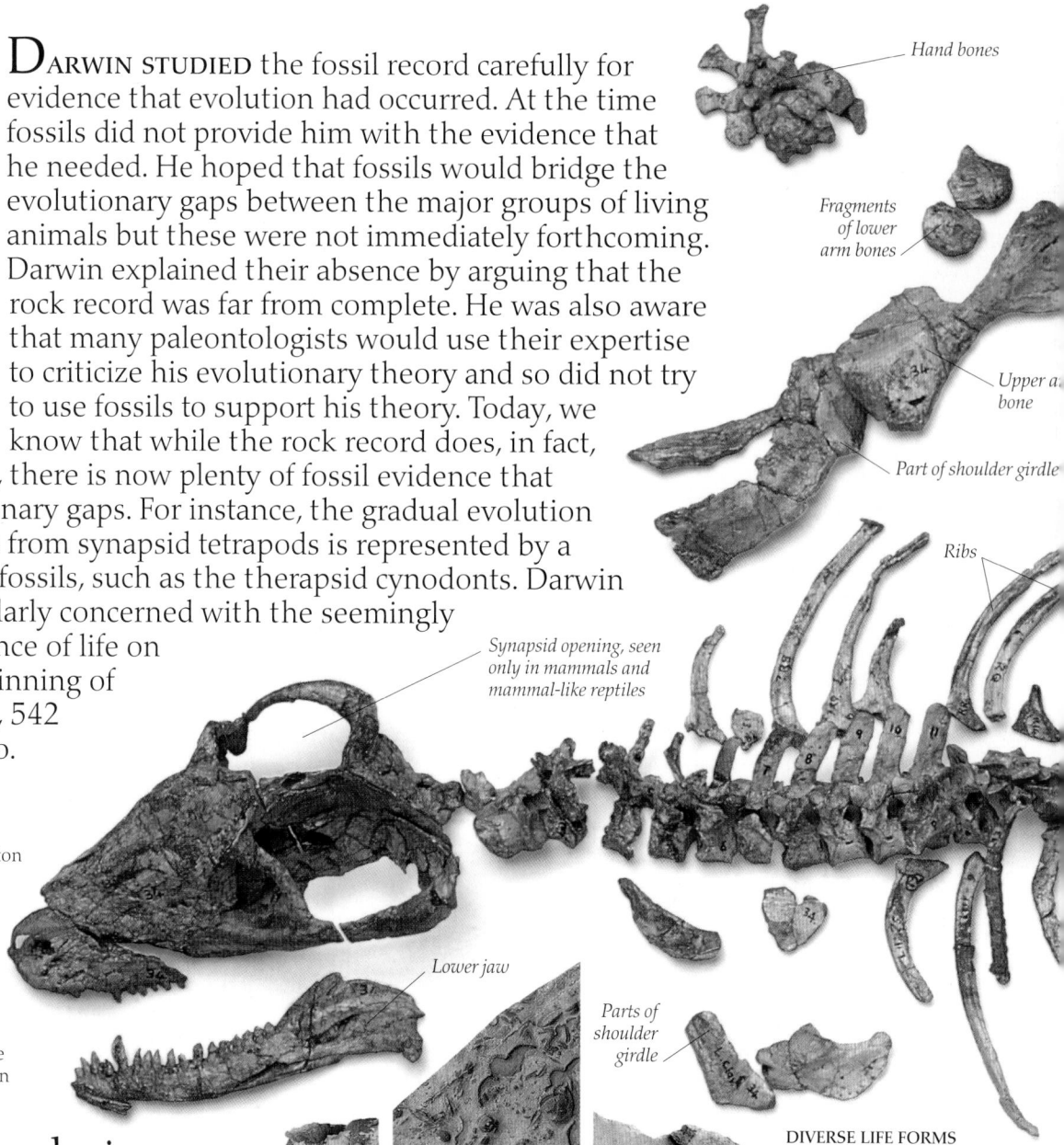

ALMOST A MAMMAL
This is the fossilized skeleton of an animal called *Procynosuchus*, a type of extinct synapsid tetrapod (a reptile with mammalian features) known as a cynodont. It was from the cynodonts that the true mammals evolved, so they have more mammalian characters than their predecessors.

Cambrian explosion

Darwin's answer to the problem of the sudden appearance of life in the Cambrian, the "Cambrian explosion," was to predict that, as more Precambrian rocks were explored, fossils would be found. This has indeed happened, and now the fossil record extends back to over 3 billion years ago, but until late Precambrian times the remains are of very primitive organisms. Even then, larger fossils, such as the soft-bodied Ediacaran fossils (p. 47), thought to be multicellular organisms, cannot yet be linked to the common early Cambrian invertebrates such as trilobites and brachiopods.

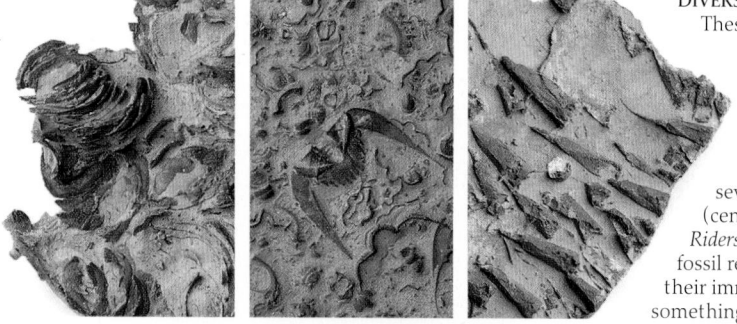

DIVERSE LIFE FORMS
These pieces of rock (left) are all from the Cambrian period, and they contain the remains of very different kinds of animals with shells—marine mollusks (far left), several kinds of trilobite, (center), and an animal called *Ridersia*. Their appearance in the fossil record is very sudden, and their immediate ancestors remain something of a mystery.

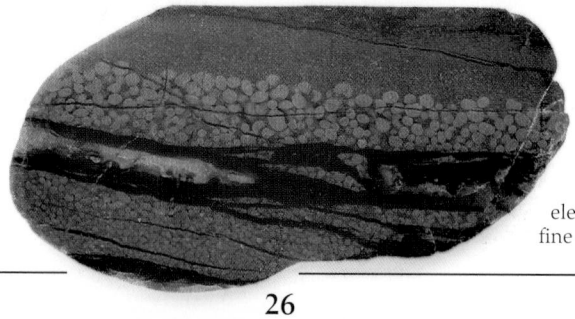

ANCIENT CELLS
The circles on this Precambrian rock are fossil colonies of cyanobacteria, or blue-green algae. To check that these were livin things, scientists can now use chemical analysis of the rock, a technique unavailabl for *Eozoon* (see right). With a scanning electron microscope, even the detail of their fine structure can now be seen.

ILED SHELLS
ese fossil cephalopods are
t a sequence of ancestors and
scendants, but they give an idea of
e evolutionary steps that led to the
htly coiled shells of the
rine animals called
monites (far right).
e earliest stage
veloped a shell
ided into
ambers, most of
hich were air-filled
d acted as a float.
is float proved
eful, but as larger
ecies evolved, a
ng buoyant shell
ust have been hard
steer when
imming. Coiling
ered a solution
this problem.

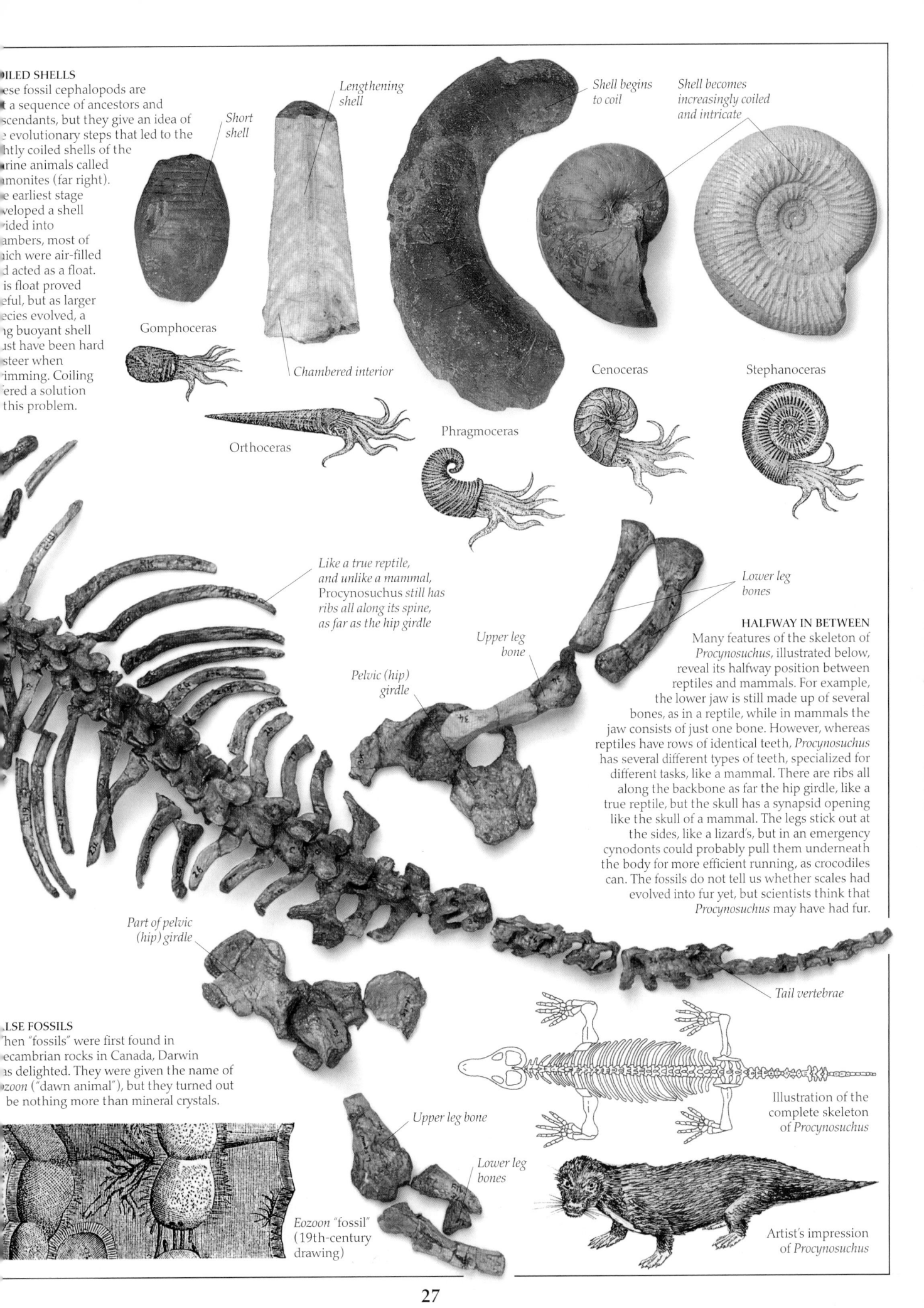

HALFWAY IN BETWEEN
Many features of the skeleton of *Procynosuchus*, illustrated below, reveal its halfway position between reptiles and mammals. For example, the lower jaw is still made up of several bones, as in a reptile, while in mammals the jaw consists of just one bone. However, whereas reptiles have rows of identical teeth, *Procynosuchus* has several different types of teeth, specialized for different tasks, like a mammal. There are ribs all along the backbone as far the hip girdle, like a true reptile, but the skull has a synapsid opening like the skull of a mammal. The legs stick out at the sides, like a lizard's, but in an emergency cynodonts could probably pull them underneath the body for more efficient running, as crocodiles can. The fossils do not tell us whether scales had evolved into fur yet, but scientists think that *Procynosuchus* may have had fur.

Illustration of the complete skeleton of *Procynosuchus*

Artist's impression of *Procynosuchus*

LSE FOSSILS
hen "fossils" were first found in
ecambrian rocks in Canada, Darwin
as delighted. They were given the name of
zoon ("dawn animal"), but they turned out
be nothing more than mineral crystals.

Eozoon "fossil" (19th-century drawing)

How old is Earth?

SLOW FORCES
The geological theories of Charles Lyell (1797–1875) were a reaction against Cuvier's catastrophe theories (p. 16). Lyell set out to explain geology using only natural forces that were still at work, rather than relying on ancient catastrophic floods as Cuvier did. Since present-day forces work very slowly, Earth must be very old, Lyell claimed.

HAVING LOOKED AT THE EVIDENCE of living things (pp. 22 and 24) and of fossils (p. 26), Darwin became convinced that evolution had occurred. At the same time, he asked himself *how* it might have occurred. In 1838 he hit on his theory of natural selection (p. 36). An obvious feature of natural selection is that it could not work quickly, because it is haphazard rather than purposeful. Darwin knew that evolution through natural selection needed an enormous amount of time, but this did not worry him, as Charles Lyell's *Principles of Geology* had convinced him that Earth was many hundreds of millions of years old. Since Lyell's time, geological research has confirmed his basic ideas, and he is known as the "father of modern geology." In 1866, however, the physicist William Thomson launched an attack on both Lyell and Darwin, claiming that Earth was, at the most, 100 million years old. Later, his figure fell to 20 million years. His calculations were based on the rate of heat loss from Earth, the present temperature of the outer crust, and the assumption that it had originally been molten. Darwin called this "one of my sorest troubles," and in later editions of *The Origin of Species* he played down natural selection, emphasizing other supposed mechanisms that he thought would work faster. Not until 1904 did Thomson's fundamental error become clear.

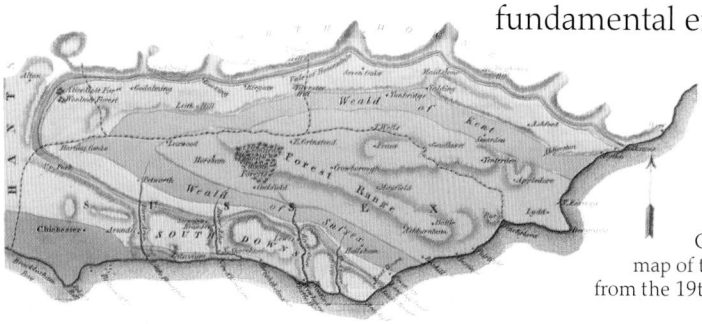

Geological map of the Weald from the 19th century

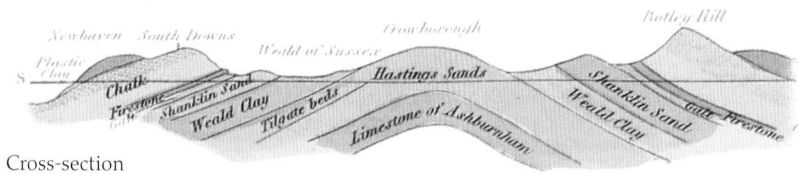

Cross-section through the Weald

THE AGE OF THE WEALD
Darwin's interest in Earth's age and how it might be estimated led to some experiments and calculations of his own. The area of southern England where he lived, called the Weald, consists of layers of sediment that were laid down under the sea, later forced upward into folds, and then eroded away. Darwin tried to work out the age of the Weald by estimating its original height and the rate of erosion. The rate was too slow, and his date of 300 million years was wildly wrong. The Wealden hills are only 20–30 million years old.

Worm stone set up at Down House, Darwin's home

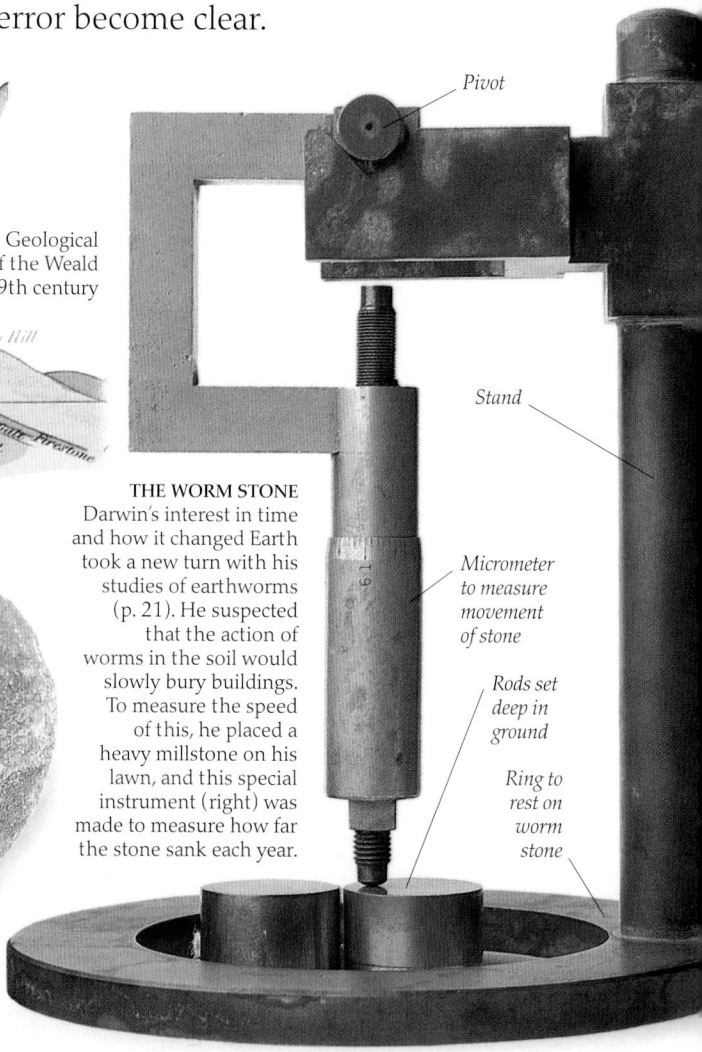

THE WORM STONE
Darwin's interest in time and how it changed Earth took a new turn with his studies of earthworms (p. 21). He suspected that the action of worms in the soil would slowly bury buildings. To measure the speed of this, he placed a heavy millstone on his lawn, and this special instrument (right) was made to measure how far the stone sank each year.

Mica window

Early Geiger counter, used to measure radioactivity

s-filled copper cylinder

Electrical supply

WRONG ANSWER
Radioactive emissions were discovered in 1896, and in 1903 Pierre Curie found that radium salts constantly give out heat, warming Earth's crust. Thomson was unaware of this, and it made his calculation of Earth's age entirely wrong. However, he made the arrogant claim that physics was a superior science to geology or biology. He thought that his one calculation could therefore overrule all the evidence collected by Lyell and by Darwin.

LORD KELVIN
William Thomson (1824–1907) was a British physicist who later became Lord Kelvin. He and his llowers had some religious otives for attacking Darwin. Like many other people, they disliked the fact that atural selection showed no purpose or direction.

Insulated handle

ASTRONOMER SON
George Darwin (1845–1913), one of Charles's 10 children, was a mathematician and astronomer. Asked by his father to check Thomson's calculations about the age of Earth, he concluded that they were mathematically correct. In later life, George Darwin was among the first to recognize that radioactivity was constantly warming Earth's crust, making Thomson's calculations meaningless.

RADIOMETRIC DATING
Radioactive elements in rocks now allow them to be dated accurately. Each radioactive element breaks down at a constant rate and always forms the same product. For example, potassium 40, found in volcanic rocks, breaks down to give argon 40. The older the rock, the more argon 40 there is. Earth's original rocks have mostly been recycled by geological processes but by measuring the age of the oldest minerals (4.4 billion years) compared with the age of meteorites (4.5 billion years), geologists have calculated Earth's age as 4.5 billion years.

MOON ROCK
Rock samples brought back from the Moon have proved useful to geologists. The Moon nd Earth were formed at the same time but, since there is no atmosphere on the Moon, there is no erosion. As predicted, geologists' calculations make Moon rock 4.5 billion years old.

DATES CONFIRMED
Meteorites were formed at the same time as Earth. Radiometric dating shows that they are 4.5 billion years old. The ages of Moon rock and meteorites have both confirmed the age of Earth that was calculated by modern geologists.

Artificial selection

IMPOSSIBLE PLANT
No one has managed yet to breed a cabbage that will grow to the size of a tree.

As PART OF HIS SEARCH for evidence about evolution, Darwin looked at domesticated animals and plants. During his lifetime, great progress had been made in developing new varieties of plants and animals through "artificial selection" or "selective breeding." This involves choosing those individuals that have the desired qualities and breeding only from them, rejecting the rest. Knowing the extent to which certain species of plants and animals had been improved in the preceding 50 years, Darwin argued that far greater changes were possible over thousands of years. This made him suspect that all breeds of sheep, for example, were descended from a single ancestor. Other naturalists disagreed—they thought that every breed must have come from a different wild species. One naturalist even suggested that there had once been *eleven* different species of wild sheep in Britain, found nowhere else in the world. Darwin pointed out how unlikely this was, since all Britain's living mammals are also found in Europe. Subsequent evidence has shown that Darwin was correct: all the different breeds of sheep were indeed developed by selective breeding from just one ancestor. The same is true of other domesticated animals, such as cows, dogs, and horses.

ROCK DOVE
This wild bird is the raw material with which pigeon breed began. All the differ pigeon breeds kept i captivity are descended from it.

DARWIN'S HOBBY
In addition to his horse, Darwin kept rabbits, chickens, ducks, and pigeons. He crossed all the different breeds of pigeon and was surprised that the young often had the same colors as the rock dove, even if neither parent had them. He realized that the rock dove must be the ancestor of them all.

PIGEON BREEDS
These are some of the many different breeds of pigeon that Darwin studied. He felt that if so much change could com about through selective breeding, then similar changes could occur through the action of natural forces alone.

ANCIENT CATTLE
Wall paintings in the tombs of ancient Egypt show cattle of many different bree Some naturalists saw such paintings as evidence that every breed was descended from a different species. After all, these breeds already existed thousands of years ago. Darwin argued that there was no reason to assume that the Egyptians wer the first farmers—selective breeding coul have begun even earlier. There is now ample evidence that his idea was correct.

GIANT DOG
The Irish wolfhound is one of the largest dogs: it can be 40 in (1 m) tall at the shoulder. The smallest, the chihuahua, may stand only 8 in (20 cm) tall. Studies of their DNA (p. 52) show that all breeds of dog are descended from the European wolf.

TAIL-FREE CAT
The Manx cat has been bred to have no tail. Cats are more difficult to breed selectively than dogs, since they like to roam at night and mate as they please. Many dog breeds were developed for useful purposes, which explains why they are more varied than cats.

BIG, BIGGER
Plant breeders can easily produce smaller or larger breeds, as these tomatoes show. The ancestral plant has been found in South America, and its tiny "tomato" is no larger than a redcurrant.

BALD DOG
The Chinese crested dog is virtually naked except for long wisps of hair on its head and tail. Breeders can alter the temperament, size, shape, and color of a dog. Its coat can be made long or short, straight or curly.

STRANGE FRUIT
Yellow tomatoes and red grapefruit are just two of the oddly colored fruits created by plant breeders. Darwin was convinced that artificial selection indicated a way in which evolution could occur—through a process that he called natural selection (p. 36).

SEEDLESS PRODUCE
In nature, fruits exist solely to distribute seeds. If there are no seeds inside it, a young fruit will normally wither and die. Breeders have managed to overcome this so that certain fruits, including bananas, some grapes, and some oranges, have no seeds.

Variation and inheritance

By 1837 Charles Darwin was certain that evolution had taken place, and he was thinking hard about the driving force behind it. For a while, he thought that Lamarck's theory about striving for change (p. 12) was the answer, but Darwin soon saw its weak points. He began taking an interest in anything that might answer this difficult question, including the breeding of crop plants, farm animals, and pets (p. 30). By questioning breeders, he learned that there were small variations between individuals, which the breeders picked out. A dog breeder would choose a feature and cross two dogs carrying it. From the puppies, those that had inherited the chosen feature would be picked out and bred. If this was repeated for several generations, the feature became more and more pronounced. Darwin saw that a similar process could occur in the wild, and he called it "natural selection" (p. 36). The three ingredients needed were variation, inheritance, and competition. Inheritance clearly took place, although Darwin never really understood how. Variation between individuals was also apparent. The third factor, competition, or "the struggle for existence," was also a fact of nature (p. 34). Competition in the wild had the same role as the dog breeder, "selecting" particular individuals for breeding and discarding others.

NO TWO THE SAME
Variation is shown in the shell colors and patterns of a seashore mollusk, *Nerites*. Not all variation is as obvious as this. There may be very small variations in size or shell thickness that are not noticeable, but that affect the animal's survival. Studies of internal features show even more differences between individuals.

Varied *Nerites* shells

MUTANT TEASEL
Fuller's teasel is a mutant form of the teasel plant that has curved spines on the seed-head instead of straight ones. Mutants were observed in the 19th century, but only in the 20th century were they studied systematically by geneticists (p. 51). Mutants arise through a sudden change, or mutation, in the DNA. This change occurs because the DNA is copied inaccurately when the reproductive cells are being produced (p. 53). Mutations are not dictated by the needs of the plant or animal. In fact, most mutations are damaging, and the mutants die young. But a few mutations are useful, and these are a major source of the variation on which natural selection operates.

Norm teas

Fuller's teasel

CHANGING BUTTERFLY
Variation is obvious in the small copper butterfly. Depending on circumstances, some may do better than others. For example, in a cool summer the darker butterflies warm up more quickly in the sun, as darker colors are better absorbers of heat.

arwin and heredity

rwin's greatest problem was heredity. He believed, wrongly, t acquired characteristics (p. 13) are inherited. But, unlike marck, Darwin did not make this the cornerstone of his ory. He thought that random variation and selection were re important. Darwin's more significant mistake was to nk that the characteristics of the parents would blend in offspring. He could see that if inheritance did involve blending of characteristics, this would be an obstacle to olution by natural selection, because if one parent had a eful new characteristic it would be diluted in the offspring. spite this, he could think of no alternative.

MILY TRAITS
eritance is obvious in st families. However, ldren often do t look like ir parents; her, they emble their ndparents or er relatives. rwin was puzzled this, but geneticists er realized that minant" and "recessive" nes (p. 51) were responsible.

Normal young

Albino young

COLOR CLUE
Darwin knew that when albino and normal mice are crossed, the colors do not blend in the young. He found several other examples, but thought they were just oddities, exceptions to the rule. In fact, they held the key to heredity, as Mendel showed (p. 51).

Normal father Dwarf Russian hamster

Albino mother Dwarf Russian hamster

The struggle for existence

MANY ANIMALS lay hundreds of eggs every year. Very few of these live to become adults—a fact that is obvious to any naturalist. The poet Alfred Lord Tennyson was aware of this when, in 1833, he wrote "Are God and Nature then at strife, That Nature lends such evil dreams? So careful of the type she seems, So careless of the single life." Unlike Tennyson, most people preferred to ignore the facts and see nature as happy and harmonious, a view made popular by the Reverend William Paley (p. 38). Darwin knew that plants and animals died in great numbers, but it took years for him to realize that this loss of life could be the driving force behind evolution. A naturalist and clergyman, the Reverend Thomas Malthus, helped him see the light. In 1798 Malthus had published *An Essay on the Principle of Population*, which argued that all living things tend to increase far faster than food supplies and that, in the case of humans, numbers are only kept in check by famine and disease. These ideas were well known to Darwin, but he did not actually read Malthus's essay until 1838. As soon as he read it, the idea of natural selection (p. 36) came to him in a flash, enabling him to make sense of all his earlier observations. Nevertheless, Darwin was always troubled by the "wasteful works of Nature." He consoled himself with the thought that "the war of nature is not incessant, that no fear is felt, that death is generally prompt, and that the vigorous, the healthy, and the happy survive and multiply."

STARVING THE POOR
The Reverend Thomas Malthus (1766–1834) was a kind man, but his essay inspired a brutal new Poor Law in Britain. The law took welfare support away from the poor unless they went into prisonlike "workhouses" where husbands and wives were separated. Feeding poor people, according to Malthus, only made poverty worse in the long run, because the poor then had more children.

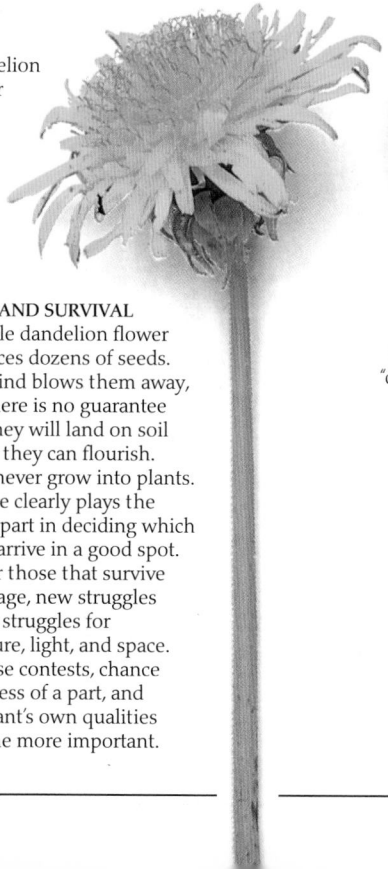

LUCK AND SURVIVAL
A single dandelion flower produces dozens of seeds. The wind blows them away, and there is no guarantee that they will land on soil where they can flourish. Most never grow into plants. Chance clearly plays the major part in deciding which seeds arrive in a good spot. But for those that survive this stage, new struggles begin: struggles for moisture, light, and space. In these contests, chance plays less of a part, and the plant's own qualities become more important.

GHTING FOR SPACE
ce most seabirds, gannets are vulnerable to predators
ien nesting, so they nest only on small, rocky islands
ere there are no rats or foxes to destroy their eggs
d young. As suitable islands are few, they become
y crowded. Competition between animals for nesting
es is another aspect of the "struggle for existence."

HUNTER AND PREY
A thin and hungry polar bear pursues a nimble arctic fox across the snow. One of the most important parts of the struggle for survival is the need to eat—and the need to keep from being eaten by others.

oglets set
ff into the
ide world

RED IN TOOTH AND CLAW
The poet Alfred Lord Tennyson wrote his poem *In Memoriam* in 1833, 25 years before Darwin published *The Origin of Species*. It includes the memorable line "Nature red in tooth and claw." This phrase later came to symbolize people's hatred for the idea of natural selection. They reacted as if Darwin had invented the struggle for existence, rather than simply described it.

ggs

Frog's spawn

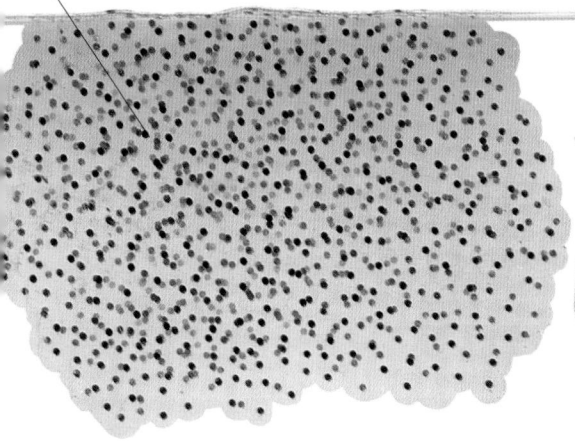

THE NUMBERS GAME
A frog can lay hundreds of eggs in a single year. If all these survived to adulthood and produced young of their own, the world would be knee-deep in frogs within 10 years. Clearly, most of them die. Some of the eggs and tadpoles are killed by fungi, some by predators. Others die from lack of food. Of the few dozen froglets that may survive each year, only one or two are likely to live long enough to breed.

Adult frog

Natural selection

GREAT MINDS
In 1858 British naturalist Alfred Wallace (1823–1913) wrote to Darwin from Malaya, asking advice on a short article he had written. To Darwin's dismay it contained the idea of natural selection. Wallace did not know that Darwin had been working on this idea for 20 years. A joint publication was hastily arranged.

HOW DOES EVOLUTION OCCUR? Charles Darwin's answer was through "natural selection." He realized that there was always some variation between individuals within a species (p. 32), so that some are a little larger, some have thicker fur, or slightly longer legs. He also realized that there is a struggle for existence (p. 34) because more individuals are born than can survive. To some extent, chance plays a part in deciding which ones survive, but the characteristics of the individual must sometimes make a difference. The animal with longer legs will run faster and thus escape a predator. The animal with thicker fur will survive a cold winter. Only those that survive have the chance to produce young ones—and that is where inheritance (p. 33) is important. If the slightly longer legs or thicker fur are passed on to some of the offspring, then more animals have those useful characteristics in the next generation. After hundreds of generations, these small changes may add up to a large and noticeable difference. Darwin proposed that this process produces adaptation (p. 38) and could also produce new species, given enough time (p. 40). The idea of natural selection came to Darwin in 1838, but he spent a further 20 years working on the idea and collecting more evidence. He was nervous about the controversies that his theory might provoke, and this too made him delay publication. Had Alfred Wallace (above left) not reached similar conclusions, Darwin might never have published at all.

WINTER KILLS
Killed by the cold and lack of food, this eagle has lost forever its chance of producing young. Another eagle, with thicker feathers, or better hunting abilities, may survive to produce chicks next spring.

Moths on light bark

Industrial pollution in 19th-century England

CONCEALING COLORS
In the 19th century a good example of natural selection occurred in the industrial regions of northern England, although no one grasped its significance at the time. The peppered moth rests on tree trunks by day. Its pale dappled wings are camouflaged against lichens growing on the trunks, and this protects the moth from insect-eating birds. Pollution kills off lichens, and as industry grew, the tree trunks turned black with soot from factory smokestacks. Dark versions of the peppered moth arose by mutation (p. 32) and were better camouflaged than the original form. Gradually, the dark forms became more and more common.

Moths on dark bark

Sexual selection

Aside from natural selection, Darwin also identified another important mechanism: sexual selection. When animals mate, they are choosy about their partners. Usually it is the female choosing the male, or males fighting to control females. Sometimes, however, females must compete for males, or both partners may be choosy. The qualities that ensure success differ widely, from physical strength to bright feathers. Only those chosen as mates pass on their characteristics to the next generation.

Single tail feather from male peacock

FIGHTING FOR MATES
Male elephant seals fight for the right to breed. On the beaches where they come to breed every year, only a few males gain a territory. These territory-holders, the ones who can fight off their rivals, herd together a "harem" of females and mate with all of them. This type of sexual selection produces great size and strength in the males. The female seals are less than half their size.

PEALING TAIL
xual selection often
olves males
racting females.
acocks display their
s to females, who
oose the best-looking
le. Bright feathers
y originally have
en favored because
ey showed that a
le was healthy,
t once this process
gins, the feathers
y become more
d more elaborate.

How does it begin?

It is easy to see how natural selection can make fur thicker or legs longer, but how does a totally new feature develop? In every case, there must be something for natural selection to work on, an existing feature that can be modified to make the new one.

Few flowers

Unfed plant

HUNGRY PLANTS
The leaves of the sundew plant have evolved to become insect traps. Most plant leaves can absorb some nutrients directly, and this must have been the starting point for the ancestor of sundews. They grew in bogs with poor soil, and small insects that happened to drown on their damp leaves would have supplied extra minerals. Natural selection would then have favored plants that increased this nutrient supply. If a plant with stickier leaves appeared, it would do better than others, because small flies would become stuck on the leaves. Darwin experimented with sundews, feeding some with small pieces of meat and keeping others unfed. Those fed on meat grew more quickly, produced more flowers, and set more seeds. He had shown that being able to trap and digest insects would be a characteristic favored by natural selection.

Flowers

Well-fed plant with plentiful flowers that will produce more seeds and thus more offspring

Vigorous growth

Meat being placed on leaf

Understanding adaptation

William Paley
(1743–1805)

MOLES HAVE STRONG, BROAD FRONT FEET for digging through soil. Duc have webbed feet for swimming. Polar bears have very thick fur. It is clear to any naturalist that all plants and animals are superbly adapted to their climate and way of life. Darwin proposed that these adaptations were an outcome of natural selection. However, there was already a powerful and popular theory about adaptation known as "natural theology." This interpreted all adaptation as evidence of the creator's handiwork. *Natural Theology, or Evidences of the Existence and Attributes of the Deity*, by the English clergyman William Paley, set out the ideas most fully. Published in 1802, Paley book was widely read. While studying for the clergy as a young mar Darwin had read and admired it, not thinking that he would one day be its greatest critic. Fortunatel the two opposing theories can each be tested against the fact: Natural theology predicts tha all adaptations should be perfect. Evolution through natural selection predicts that they should be influenced by (and often limited by) the past.

PALEY'S WATCH
William Paley began *Natural Theology* with an example to prove his basic point. He imagined himself walking across a heath and finding a watch among the stones. Unlike the stones, the watch has moving parts that work together for a purpose. The existence of the watch would prove that there was a watchmaker. Paley drew a parallel between a watch and an animal. Just as the watch proved the existence of a watchmaker, so an animal (or a plant) proved the existence of a Creator. By studying natural history, the nature of God could be better understood.

What purpose?

Inspired by natural theology, naturalists set out to find God's intended "purpose" for each living thing, a difficult task, especially in the case of pests such as rats and fleas. In Darwin's view, the only "purpose" of any creature is a private one—to survive and produce young. If it does this, it has succeeded in passing on its characteristics to the next generation.

Faces of leaf-nosed bats

ECHOES OF CREATION?
Bats navigate by making high-pitched sounds and listening for the echoes. Some have elaborate nose-leaves to channel the sound. Can such devices be produced by natural selection, or must there be a "watchmaker," a creator? The fact is that there are many simple versions of this "radar" among bats, and a range of intermediate forms leading up to the most complex ones. This has convinced biologists that such features can, and have, evolved.

European mole

Strong arm for digging

Long, thin hand and finger bones support wing

SAME BONES
The bat's spreading wing and the mole's stubby digging arm have the same set of bones, as do the arms of all mammals (p. 23). This astonishing similarity only makes sense if Darwin was correct and they come from the same distant ancestor.

Leaf-nosed bat

ar from perfect

ording to Natural Theology, the adaptations iving things should be perfect. According to win, adaptations are always restricted the ancestry of the plant or animal, ause natural selection can only work the raw material available. If the raw terial is not ideal for the purpose, or natural ection has not had long enough to work, adaptations will be less-than-perfect.

rs occasionally attack er animals

THE PANDA'S THUMB
Bears are mostly omnivores, and their paws have five very short "fingers." Giant pandas, descended from bears, eat bamboo shoots and need a thumb to hold them. In fact, they have evolved one, but it is a short, imperfect thumb jutting out from the wrist. It seems that the bear's paw was too specialized for natural selection to "reverse" the basic plan and make a true thumb. Instead, the panda's false thumb has grown from a bone in the wrist.

Panda's paw

False thumb

STILL ADAPTING
Many people suffer from backaches, or problems with their hips, knees, or feet, while pain in the arms is rare. In Darwin's terms, this makes sense. Humans are unusual among mammals in standing upright. The fossil evidence suggests that we only began to do so between 5 and 8 million years ago. The human back and legs have not yet had time to adapt fully.

ate

GATE BIRD PUZZLE
win pointed out that n frigate birds and and geese have bed feet, yet neither s into the water. explained their as a leftover from ir past, both ng descended n waterbirds. ney were igned by a tor, Darwin ndered, why they have se useless tures?

King penguin

Giant panda

Human spine

DESIGN FAULT
Loons, or divers, can scarcely walk on land (below), because their legs are set so far back on the body. Most diving birds have the legs set far back, because this is the best position for efficient swimming. The penguin (left) has solved the problem of walking by adopting an upright stance. For the loon, upright walking may evolve in time. A "watchmaker" might have made the loon more mobile on land by standing it upright, or by adding another pair of legs near the middle.

Red-throated diver

How new species are formed

ALTHOUGH DARWIN called his book *The Origin of Species*, he said very little about how new species might arise. In fact, he called this the "mystery of mysteries." Today, the process is better understood, although there are still disagreements about the details. In general, most new species arise when a population becomes cut off from the rest of its kind, especially if it then lives in conditions that differ from those of the parent species. This might happen, for example, when birds are blown off course and reach distant islands (p. 25) or cross a mountain range. Sheer distance can also be a physical barrier, as in the case of a ring species (below). Under new conditions, or simply because they are isolated, the population may begin to evolve in a different direction and may develop into a new race or subspecies. In time, that subspecies can change so much and become so different from the rest of its species that the two can no longer interbreed. Once this happens, they are two distinct species. Occasionally, a new species may arise in other ways, without any geographical isolation.

THE COMTE DE BUFFON
Georges Buffon (1707–1788) of France was the first to define a species as a group of living things that can all potentially interbreed with each other, but not with members of other species.

Herring gull (*Larus argentatus argentatus*)

Lesser black-backed gull (*Larus fuscus graellsi*)

ONE SPECIES OR TWO?
The herring gull (left) and the lesser black-backed gull (right) are descended from gulls that lived in eastern Siberia. These ancestral gulls spread out to both east and west. In time, the two lines of migration met on the other side of the globe, over northern Europe. The two ends of this circle are the herring gull and the lesser black-backed gull. These birds have changed so much from their common ancestor that they do not interbreed, except very rarely.

Larus argentatus vegae

Larus argentatus birulaii

North Pole

Larus fuscus antellus

Larus fuscus heuglini

Larus argentatus smithsonianus

Larus argentatus omissus

Larus fuscus fuscus

Larus argentatus argentatus

Larus fuscus graellsi

RING SPECIES
Each of the different subspecies of herring gull interbreeds with its neighbors, as do the different subspecies of lesser black-backed gull. In eastern Siberia, the herring gulls interbreed with neighbors that are called black-backed gulls, but could just as well be called herring gulls. These gulls form a "ring species" and show how new species can arise through accumulated small changes.

solating mechanisms

new species may develop in isolation, but often it moves ck into the area where the "parent" species lives. The two ecies may still be similar enough to mate and produce ung, although these hybrid offspring are infertile (unable have young themselves). For the parents, producing such ybrid is a waste of time and energy, so it pays them to cognize their own species. They do so using signals such smell, sound, color, or behavior. These signals, which keep ecies apart, are called "isolating mechanisms."

Chiff-chaff

Wood warbler

Willow warbler

T ONE, BUT THREE
e English naturalist Gilbert White 720–1793) was the first to notice that e chiff-chaff, the willow warbler, and the ood warbler were three different species, d not just one. The wood warbler is ghtly larger and brighter in color, t the chiff-chaff and willow warbler ok almost exactly the same. The ngs of these three, however, are distinctly different. For the birds, e songs are used by the female to ect a mate, so in this way they as an isolating mechanism, parating the otherwise milar species.

CHOOSING A MATE
utterflies, which fly by day, recognize potential mates y their patterns and colors. Moths, which fly by night, rely more on scent. For many species, there are also internal mechanisms that prevent fertilization between different species. These are especially important in plants.

South American Sweet Oil butterflies mating

GETTING IT RIGHT
These butterflies have made the right choice of mate, but this is not always the case. Mistakes are occasionally made because isolating mechanisms, like adaptations (p. 39), are a product of evolutionary change and are not necessarily perfect. For example, a horse may mate with a donkey, producing a mule, which is infertile.

Asian swallowtails mating

PERFUMED PARTNERS
Mice and many other mammals recognize their own species by characteristic scents. In some species, specific courtship rituals are performed. These are used to confirm that the correct choice of partner has been made.

KEPT APART
Theodosius Dobzhansky (1900–1975) worked with T. H. Morgan on fruit flies (p. 51) and helped in the synthesis of genetics and evolutionary theory. He coined the term "isolating mechanisms" for the biological barriers that discourage crossing between different species.

Fossil intermediates

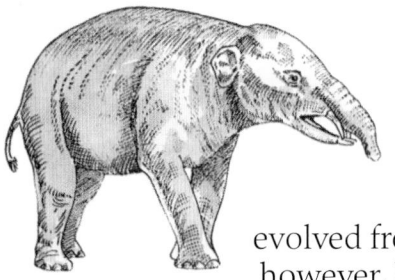

ANCIENT ELEPHANT
Together with other fossils, the 35-million-year-old fossil *Phiomia* (pictured in this artist's impression) shows how elephants, mammoths, and mastodons evolved from relatively small, hippolike animals.

LIKE LIVING INTERMEDIATES (p. 42), fossil intermediates can reveal how new groups evolved from existing ones. They are not a perfect guide, however, because the full set of intermediates is very rarely found. It has been estimated that only one fossil species is found for every 20,000 species that have lived, so the chances of finding an actual ancestor of a living group is very small. The most that scientists can hope for is to find a fossil species that was related to such an ancestor. This means that some guesswork must be used in reconstructing past events. However, the guesses made are based on a great deal of careful study of the fossils, and of living things. All ideas about how things evolved are repeatedly tested and questioned by other scientists. When new fossils are found, they are used to test existing theories about the past and may confirm or disprove those theories. Among the fossils that have helped to reveal the course of evolution are those of early frogs (below). Fossil frogs show that broad skulls came before features such as very long legs. Broad skulls and mouths are typical of animals that catch fast-moving prey under water, so it seems that this led the way in frog evolution.

Artist's impression of *Mia* from 50 mill years a

HALFWAY THERE
Fossil skeletons of *Miacis* show th it was on the evolutionary line leading to martens and stoats. Fos of *Miacis* have been found in coal seams, the remains of ancient den forests, in Germany.

Artist's impressio 20-million-y old *Enaliar*

ANCIENT SEA DOG
Another fossil, *Enaliarctos*, reveals how doglike ancestors evolved in sea lions. It probably fed in the sea, but spent more time on land than living sea lions.

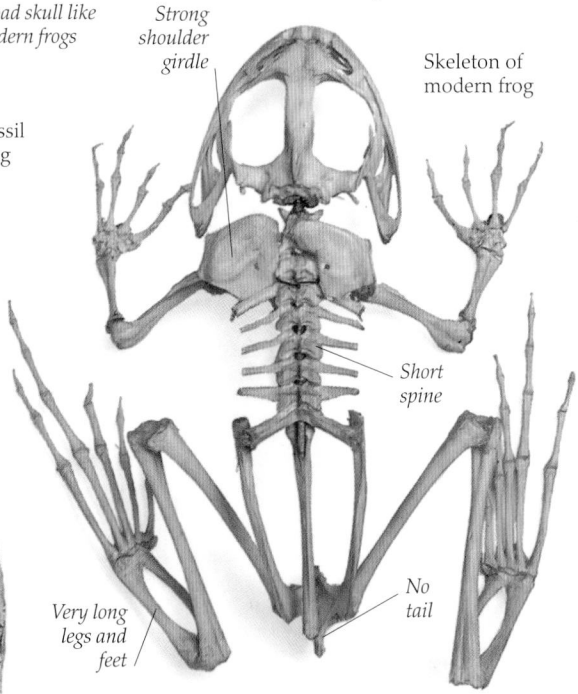

GREAT LEAP FORWARD
Frogs have specialized skeletons, allowing them to make huge jumps. They evolved from newtlike animals that swam with a side-to-side motion as fish do. On land, they walked. Fossil frogs suggest that jumping did not evolve directly from walking. Early frogs may have begun by catching mobile prey in water. This created a need for fast swimming, which they achieved by kicking with both hind legs at once. Longer legs developed, paving the way for jumping.

tholestes—small
saur with skeleton
h like that of
aeopteryx

M DINOSAUR TO BIRD
fossil *Archaeopteryx*, the oldest known bird,
atomically very similar to small two-legged
saurs such as *Compsognathus* but has
ner impressions on its wings. *Archaeopteryx*
d fly, if not very efficiently. In the late 19th
ury Thomas Henry Huxley realized that its
bination of reptilian features, such as a
bony tail, and bird features, such as the
ged structure of its arms, represented one
e first fossil vindications of Darwin's
ory of evolution. The discovery of feathered
saurs has put the evolution of birds
dinosaurs beyond dispute.

ist's impression of
chaeopteryx gliding

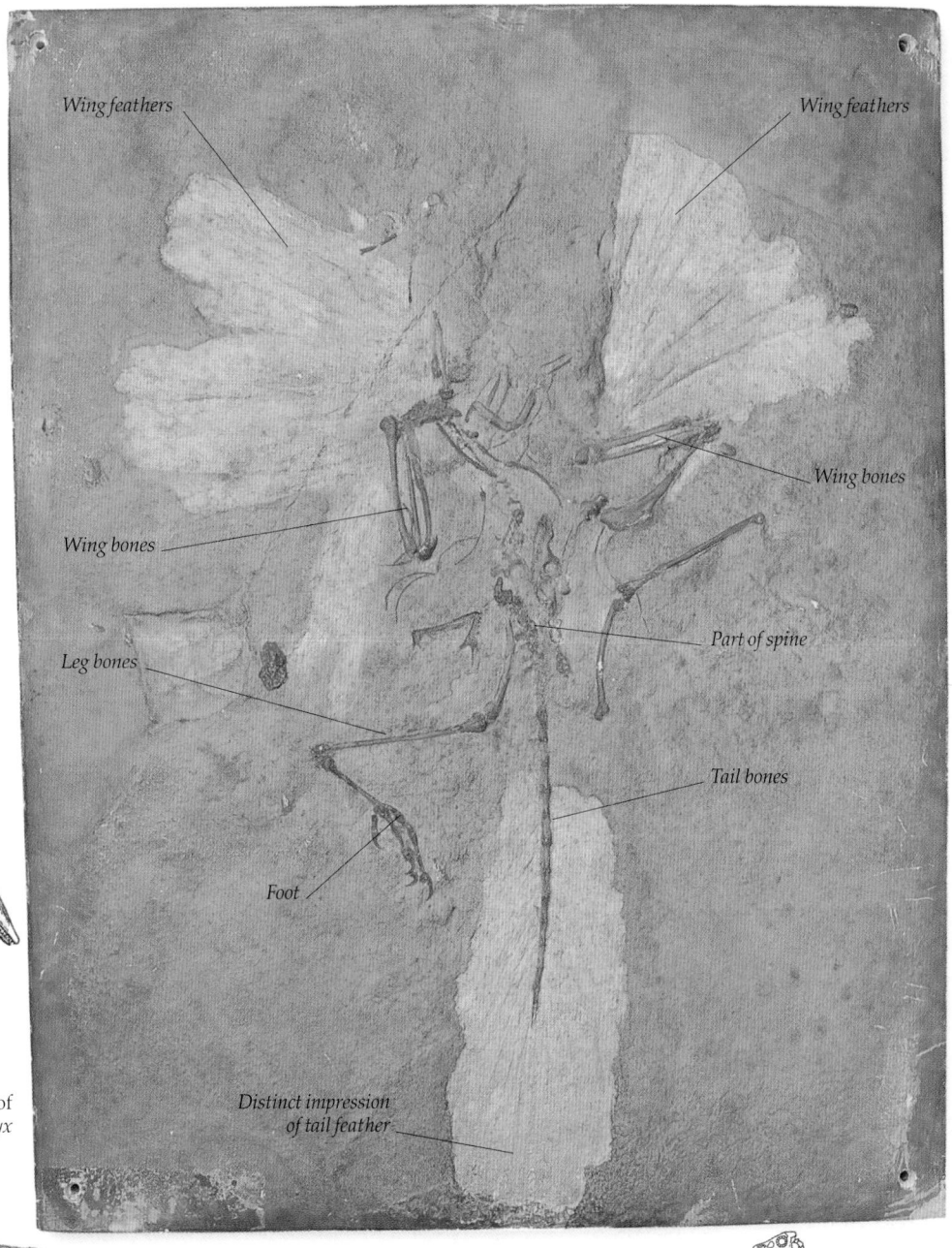

Fossil of *Archaeopteryx*

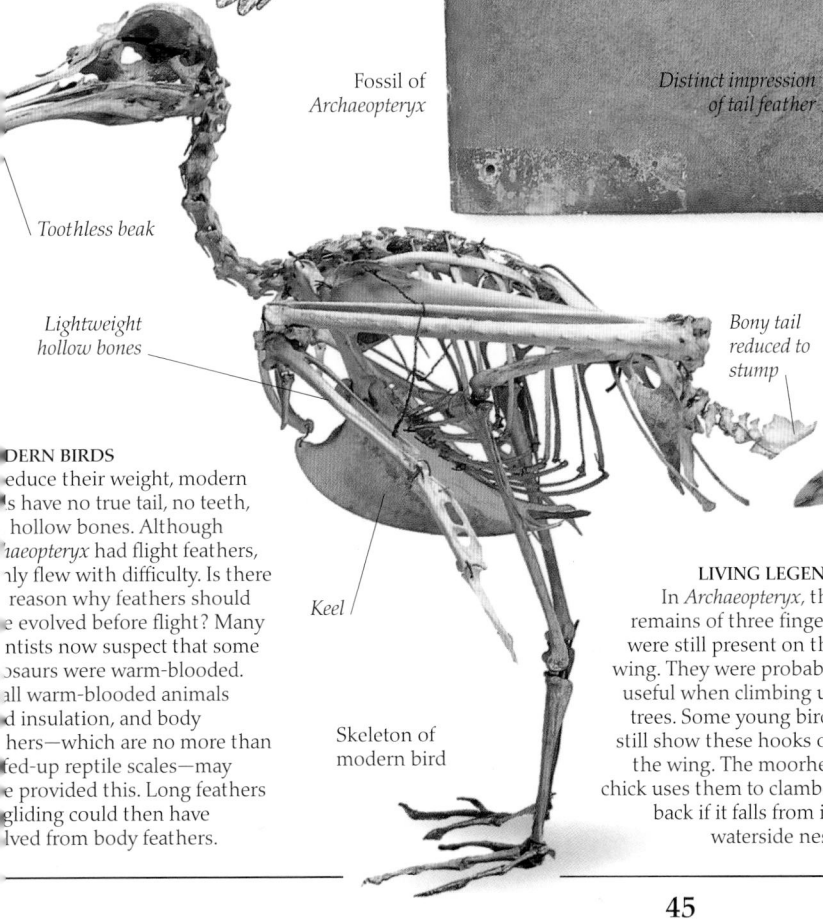

Skeleton of modern bird

DERN BIRDS
educe their weight, modern
s have no true tail, no teeth,
hollow bones. Although
aeopteryx had flight feathers,
nly flew with difficulty. Is there
reason why feathers should
e evolved before flight? Many
ntists now suspect that some
saurs were warm-blooded.
all warm-blooded animals
d insulation, and body
hers—which are no more than
fed-up reptile scales—may
e provided this. Long feathers
gliding could then have
lved from body feathers.

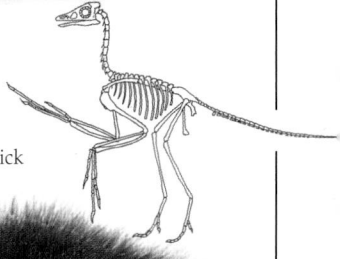

Dinosaurlike skeleton of *Archaeopteryx*

Moorhen chick

LIVING LEGEND
In *Archaeopteryx*, the remains of three fingers were still present on the wing. They were probably useful when climbing up trees. Some young birds still show these hooks on the wing. The moorhen chick uses them to clamber back if it falls from its waterside nest.

Jumps and gaps

THE CAMBRIAN EXPLOSION
This fossil arthropod from the Burgess shale in the Canadian Rocky Mountains belongs to the Cambrian period at the start of the Paleozoic era (below), when many new animals suddenly appeared. No definite ancestors have yet been identified.

WHILE THERE ARE MANY INTERMEDIATE forms found in the fossil record (pp. 26 and 44), there are also many jumps and gaps. Evolutionists can now explain some of these, but not all. The most puzzling is the sudden appearance of many new and fairly complex animals in the Cambrian period (p. 26). This is still not fully understood, but scientists continue to investigate the issue. A second puzzle, the dramatic changes in fossils at the end of the Paleozoic era and the Mesozoic era, are now fairly well explained (below). A third problem is the lack of intermediates that bridge the gap between many groups, especially invertebrates. It seems that intermediate forms are relatively rare, perhaps because changes occur rapidly, and only in one small area of the world. This would mean that few intermediates become fossils. As a comparison, if a multistory parking garage were "fossilized" by a fall of volcanic ash, there would be plenty of cars fossilized on each level, but the chances of a car being fossilized while driving up from one level to the next would be relatively small.

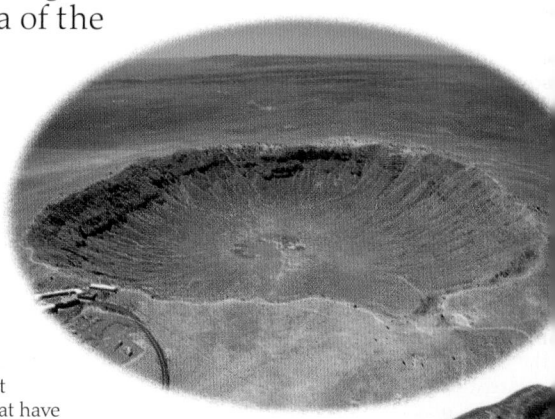

END OF THE MESOZOIC
The Arizona meteorite crater is a recent example of the many impact events that have affected Earth and its life. The Mesozoic Era ended 65 million years ago with a major extinction event, coinciding with a giant 7-mile (11-km) wide meteorite crashing into the Gulf of Mexico. Life was devastated and groups such as the ammonites and dinosaurs died out, except for the small, feathered dinosaurs we know as birds.

CHANGING ERAS
As the early geologists noted (p. 16), the fossils from one geological period differ from those of another. The differences between the three major eras (Precambrian, Paleozoic, and Mesozoic) which each include several geological periods (p. 60), are even greater, as these three pieces of fossil-bearing rock show. The major differences between the fossils from successive eras are due to mass extinctions.

2 MESOZOIC
Triassic rock, containing ammonites, belongs to the Mesozoic era, the age of dinosaurs. Both dinosaurs and ammonites became extinct at the end of this era, 65 million years ago, when some 60 percent of species died out.

Rock containing fossilized sea shells and remains of trilobites

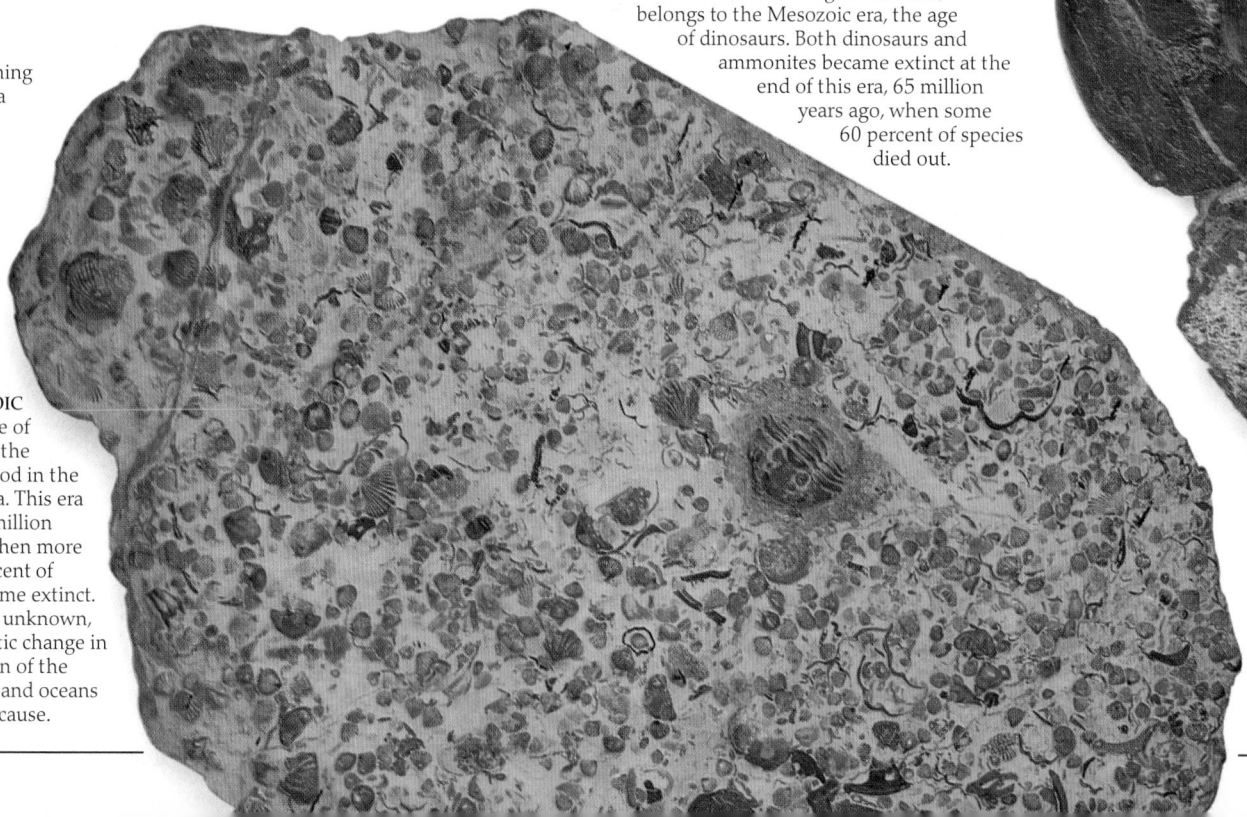

1 PALEOZOIC
This piece of rock is from the Silurian period in the Paleozoic era. This era ended 251 million years ago, when more than 90 percent of species became extinct. The cause is unknown, but a dramatic change in the condition of the atmosphere and oceans is the likely cause.

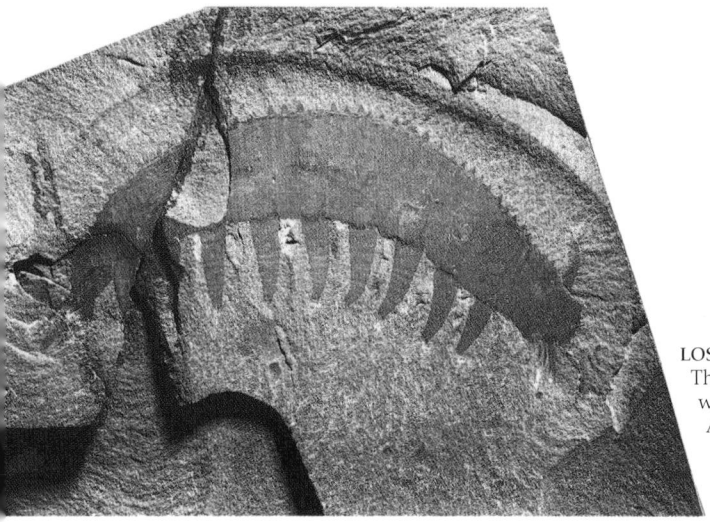

URGESS BEAST
ere is no reason to doubt that mbrian animals, like this one m the Burgess shale, are scended from Precambrian e. All living things are ited by the same basic emistry and the same netic code (p. 55).

ONG GONE
ese soft-bodied eatures from late ecambrian rock (right) red just before the mbrian, and are known the Ediacara fauna. ost scientists think that they are unlikely ancestors for the Cambrian animals, but some disagree.

LOST AND FOUND
The coelacanth is a fish that was thought to be extinct. All the known fossils were more than 200 million years old. Then, in 1938, a live coelacanth was fished out of the ocean. If the coelacanth could survive for 200 million years without leaving any fossils, it is not surprising that some steps in the evolution of life are not recorded.

HARD TO RECOGNIZE
Even when intermediate forms do become fossils, they may not be recognized as such. The dipper (below) dives for its food, but looks like a land bird. Though it may evolve adaptations for underwater life, it has none yet. If dippers were extinct, no one would guess from their fossils how they had lived.

Fossil imprints of soft-bodied animals (left and below) from the Ediacara Hills in Australia

3 CENOZOIC
This rock (below right), bearing fossil fish, comes from the Tertiary period, part of the Cenozoic era. During the Cenozoic, which is still in progress, mammals and birds have taken over the many vacant slots left by the disappearance of the dinosaurs. After mass extinctions, some surviving species evolve into new forms that repopulate Earth.

ssil
mmonite

Triassic rock

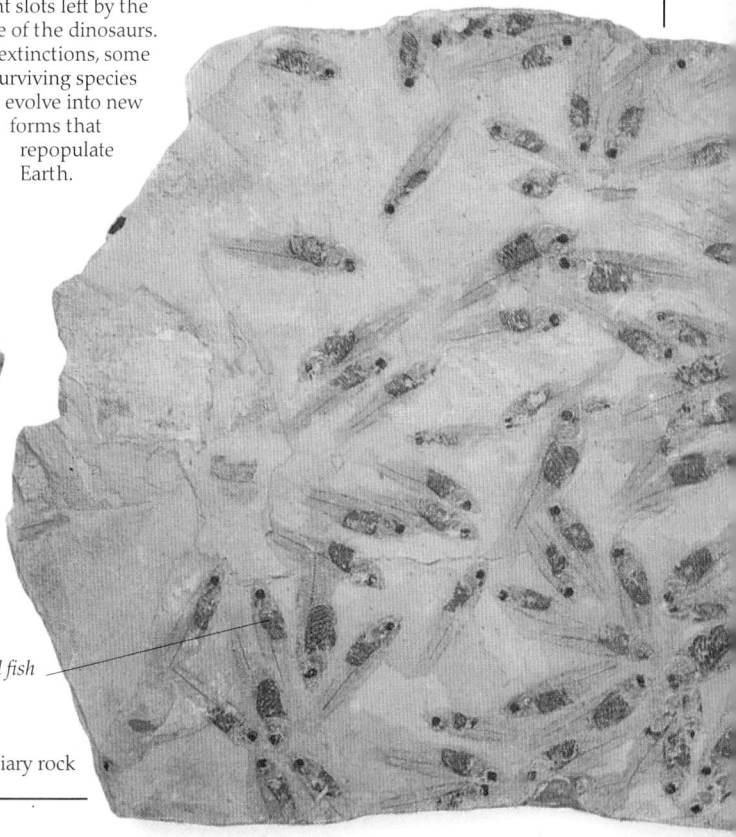

Fossil fish

Tertiary rock

Ladders and branches

ALL FOR PROGRESS
Ernst Haeckel (1834–1919) developed the idea of "evolution as progress" to its fullest extent. He believed that nature had been deliberately moving toward a final goal: human beings. The more that is discovered about what happened in the past, the less this idea makes sense.

IN 19TH-CENTURY Europe and North America the "Industrial Revolution" was changing everyone's lives. Towns were growing rapidly, a network of railroads was spreading, and new factories were drawing thousands of workers from the countryside to the cities. Almost every aspect of social life was in a process of change. Most people, especially those in power, believed that all these changes amounted to "Progress," and that progress must be good. Evolution was a controversial idea for religious reasons, and linking it to progress made it far more acceptable. Darwin himself refrained from making this connection because he knew that the reality of evolution did not quite fit in with such ideas. For example, many types of bacteria have stayed small and simple for billions of years without "progressing" to become larger or more complex. This is also true of many other living things whose evolutionary history is more like a branching bush of diversification than a ladder of constant improvement. However, Darwin did not try to contradict two of his followers, Thomas Huxley and Ernst Haeckel, both of whom presented evolution in terms of progress. This rapidly became the popular view, and the idea is still widespread today.

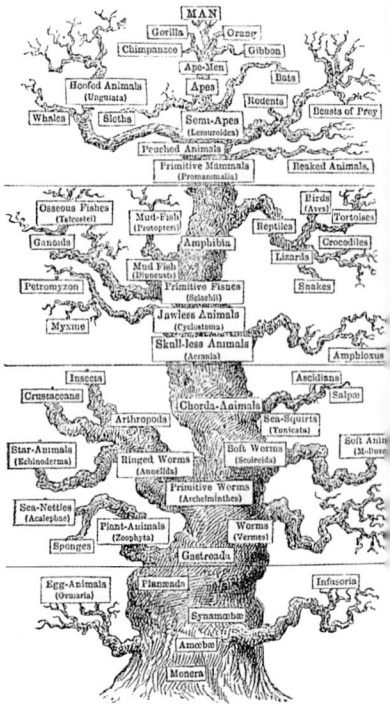

ECHOES OF THE PAST
As well as putting humans at the top, Haeckel's tree contains another of his theories: recapitulation. He believed that as an embryo developed it went through all the evolutionary stages of its ancestor. The five "ancestors" at the bottom of the tree trunk are based on the very early stages of development of an embryo.

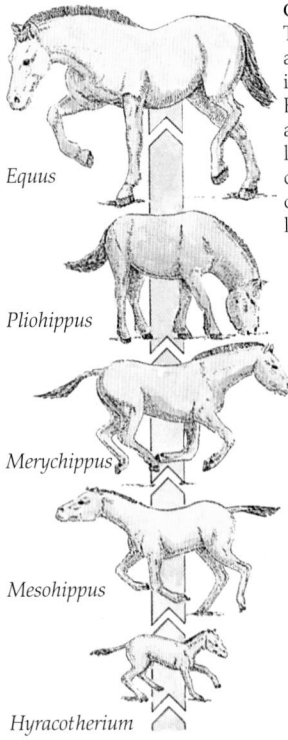

GALLOPING UP
The evolution of the horse is often shown by a diagram such as this (left). Although the fossils of all these ancestors have indeed been found, this "ladder" gives a false picture. Evolution does not go in straight lines, and it is not always a steady march of progress from small-and-simple to large-and-complicated. A more realistic image is a densely branching bush (below). There have been dozens of species, most of which have died out, leaving just wild horses, donkeys, and zebras.

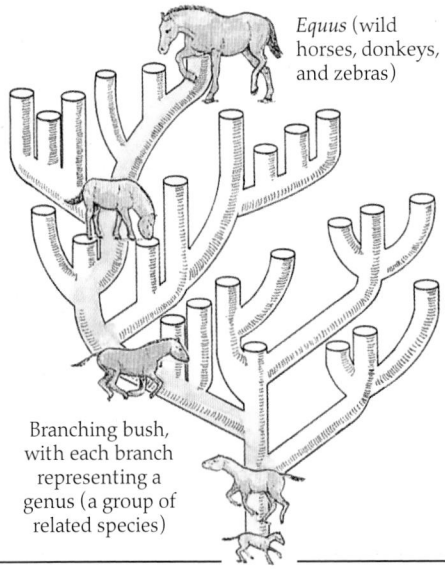

Branching bush, with each branch representing a genus (a group of related species)

"DARWIN'S BULLDOG"
Thomas H. Huxley (1825–1895) was a young, energetic English scientist who took up the cause of evolution in many public debates. He fought on behalf of Darwin, who preferred to keep out of the public eye. However, Huxley was inspired by Haeckel, and he distorted Darwin's ideas with notions of "progress."

OUR MISSING TAIL *(belo*
The mistaken idea of recapitulati contains a grain of truth. Young embry do resemble the embryos of relat animals. For example, at about fo weeks of age the human emb (below) has a set of parallel groo like those that lead to gill slits fish. It also has a tail at this sta which is later lost. The emb does develop in a way t sometimes echoes evolutionary past, but it do not reenact every step its evolution Haeckel suggest

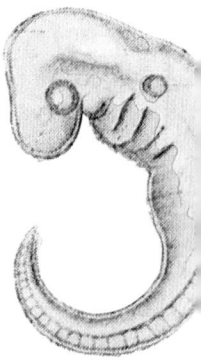

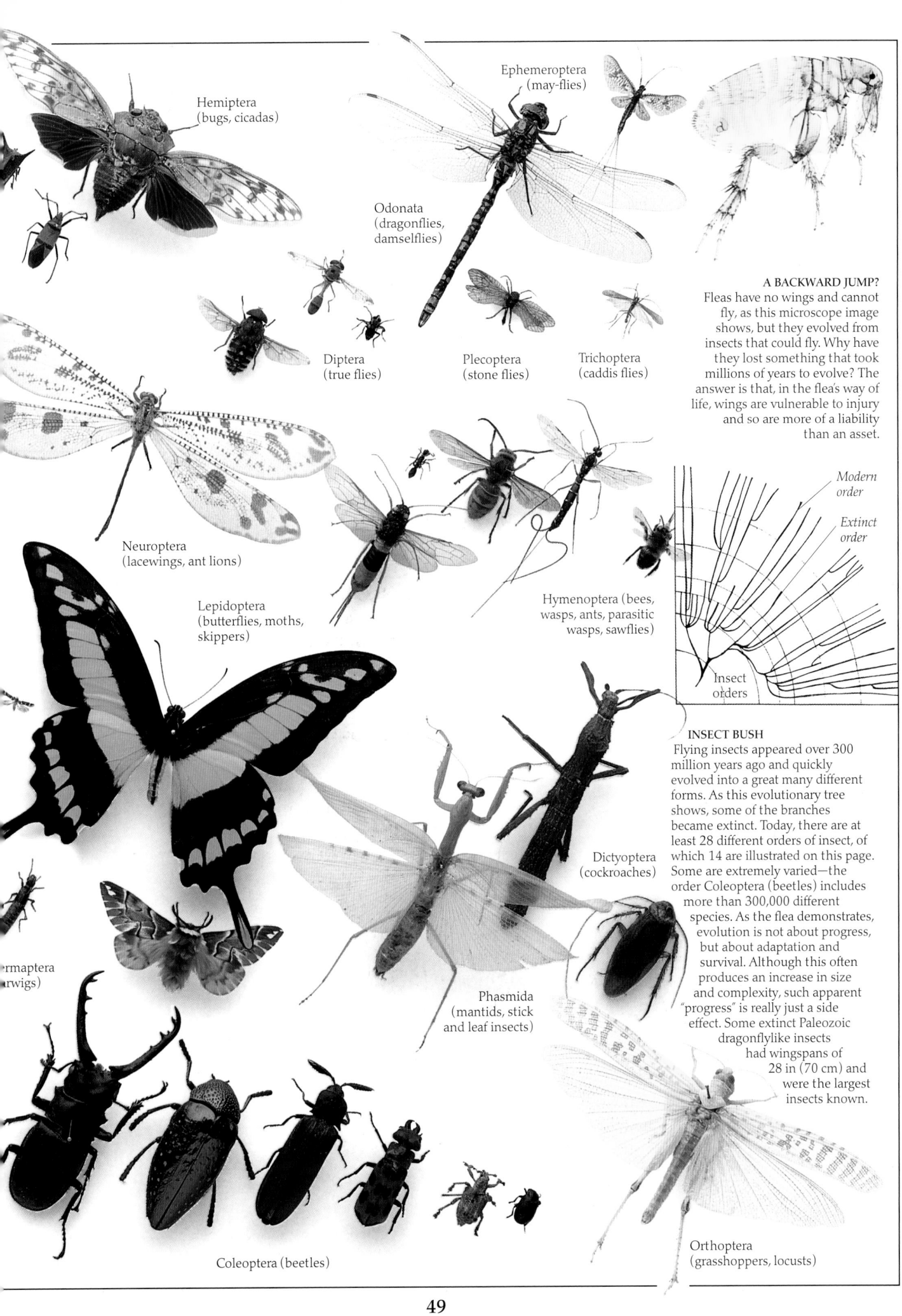

A BACKWARD JUMP?
Fleas have no wings and cannot fly, as this microscope image shows, but they evolved from insects that could fly. Why have they lost something that took millions of years to evolve? The answer is that, in the flea's way of life, wings are vulnerable to injury and so are more of a liability than an asset.

INSECT BUSH
Flying insects appeared over 300 million years ago and quickly evolved into a great many different forms. As this evolutionary tree shows, some of the branches became extinct. Today, there are at least 28 different orders of insect, of which 14 are illustrated on this page. Some are extremely varied—the order Coleoptera (beetles) includes more than 300,000 different species. As the flea demonstrates, evolution is not about progress, but about adaptation and survival. Although this often produces an increase in size and complexity, such apparent "progress" is really just a side effect. Some extinct Paleozoic dragonflylike insects had wingspans of 28 in (70 cm) and were the largest insects known.

Gregor Mendel

GREGOR MENDEL
The talented and intelligent son of poor peasants, Mendel could continue his science studies only by entering the local monastery. Many of his fellow monks were enthusiastic scientists.

GREGOR MENDEL (1822–1884) was a monk and a physicist. Some of his fellow monks were crop breeders, and he began investigating heredity to help them to improve their crops. Being a physicist, he looked for simple laws that could be expressed mathematically, and this happened to be a good way of approaching heredity. By an inspired guess, Mendel chose to study "either/or" characteristics, such as seed color in peas. Others scientists were looking at characteristics that appear to blend in the offspring, such as size. Though these are more common, they are far more difficult to study. Mendel's results, published in 1865, were not understood until 1900, when scientists made the same discoveries again. "Mendelism" was born, and in 1909 the word "gene" was coined for his hereditary particles (p. 52). At first Mendelism seemed to oppose Darwinism, because "either/or" characteristics would not create the small variations on which natural selection could work. In the 1920s it was realized that most characteristics are governed by dozens of genes, each with small effects that can add up to a large effect. The many genes controlling a characteristic such as size can provide small variations, but each gene behaves in exactly the same way as a gene for an "either/or" characteristic. The ideas of Mendelism clearly supported Darwin, and they were combined in a new theory—neo-Darwinism.

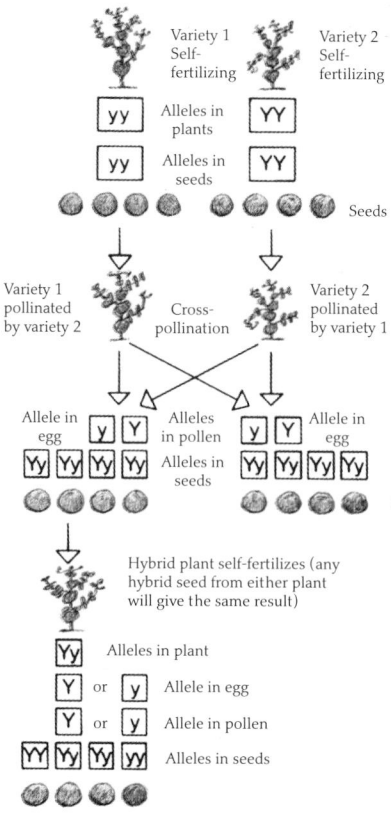

MINIATURE TREES
Bonsai trees, like trees grown in harsh natural conditions, show how much external forces influence a characteristic such as size. The tree's genes (its "genotype") provide the raw material, but what happens to the tree helps to shape its actual form (the "phenotype"). To study heredity, it is important to look at characteristics that are not affected by external factors, or to keep the external factors exactly the same.

Tree stunted by severe pruning

Bonsai yew, less than 1 ft (30 cm) t

A branch of normal yew, a tree that grows to a height of 80 ft (25 m)

inding genes

ndel worked with plant ieties (different types hin a species). He crossed ieties that had distinct, ntrasting characteristics, h as seed color. His ults showed that heredity s not blending, but olved discrete units, w called genes.

SSING PEAS *(left)*
ndel crossed a green-seeded ety of pea with a yellow one. a flowers normally fertilize mselves, but they can be fertilized hand with pollen from another nt.) All the seeds from the cross e yellow. These seeds were nted, and the plants were allowed elf-fertilize. They produced ow and green peas, in a ratio of . This ratio reveals what is pening inside the plants. As ndel realized, there must be editary particles (now called es) that do not divide or blend. In s case, there is a single gene for d color, but two different versions alleles) of the gene. One allele es for yellow, the other for green. h seed carries two alleles, and if y are of different types then the d is yellow: the allele for yellow lled the dominant) masks the ct of the allele for green (called recessive). Each seed receives allele from the pollen and one le from the egg.

H. MORGAN (1866–1945)
omas Hunt Morgan began work fruit flies in 1907. By 1911 he had own that genes were located on the romosomes. His work helped lead to e realization that most characteristics controlled by many genes.

Red ink

Blue ink

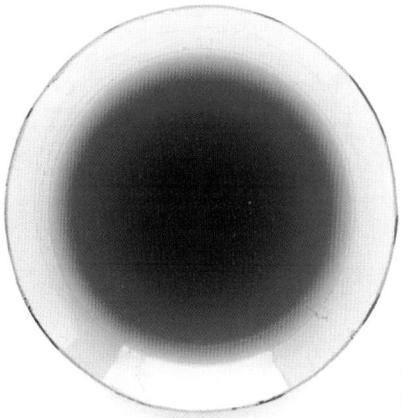

Red and blue inks mixed to produce purple

BLENDING QUALITIES
If a plant variety with red flowers is crossed with another variety having blue flowers, the offspring usually have purple flowers. It appears that the effect is like that of mixing inks.

Inks cannot be separated

SEPARATING PARTICLES *(below)*
Heredity actually depends on particles called genes, but for most characteristics dozens of genes are involved, not just one as for the color of peas. Each gene has a small effect, but together they can add up to a large effect. The mixture of red and blue beads shows how the combined action of many genes can give a result that resembles blending inheritance, but this result is only superficial. By breeding from the purple-flowered hybrids, it is possible to get blue plants and red plants again. Like beads, the genes can be separated out again.

Red beads

Blue beads

Red and blue beads mixed to produce purple; each bead represents a single allele of one gene for flower color

Unlike inks, different colored beads can be separated out again

BRED IN BOTTLES
Fruit flies *(Drosophila)* are far easier to study than plants. They can be kept in bottles, they breed quickly, and they often undergo spontaneous changes (called mutations) in their genes. Through his work on these flies, Morgan managed to locate each gene at a specific site, or "locus," on a chromosome. Chromosomes are situated in the nucleus, at the center of every cell.

Normal fly

Tiny mutant fruit fly

This "White Miniature Forked" has three mutations

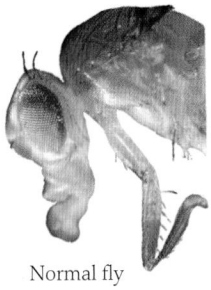

Normal fly

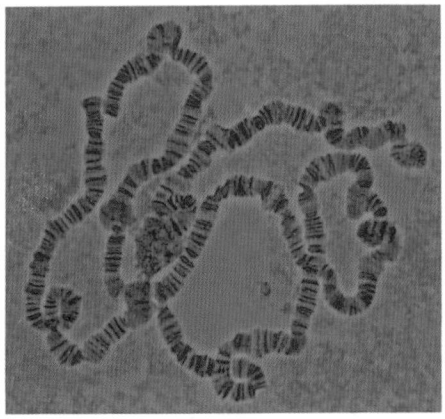

SEEING GENES
Fruit flies offer an added bonus to geneticists—they have giant chromosomes in their salivary glands, and because of their size these can be studied more easily than normal chromosomes. Each band on the chromosomes corresponds to an individual gene site, or "locus." Genes are now known to consist of DNA (p. 52).

Solving the DNA puzzle

X-RAY VISION
Rosalind Franklin (1921–1958) studied crystals of DNA using X-ray diffraction. The way in which the crystals scatter the X-rays reveals the structure and chemistry of the molecules in the crystal. Rosalind Franklin's images confirmed earlier theories about DNA, that its molecule is indeed a double helix.

By the 1920s, it was clear that the chromosomes (p. 51) carry the genes. Chromosomes were found to contain both deoxyribonucleic acid (DNA) and protein, and no one knew which was the hereditary material. James Watson (b. 1928) and Francis Crick (1916–2004) guessed that it was DNA; they hoped that, by figuring out its structure, they could understand heredity. They had seen X-ray images of DNA, and they knew the shape and chemistry of its various components. Using all this information, they tried to work out the structure by building models. Success came in 1953 and, as they had hoped, the structure revealed how heredity worked. The molecule is like a ladder twisted into a double helix. The rungs of the ladder are made up of chemical compounds called bases, two per rung (called a base pair). There are four different types of base (adenine, cytosine, thymine, and guanine). The breakthrough for Watson and Crick was the realization that adenine could pair only with thymine, and guanine could pair only with cytosine. They saw that this would enable DNA to divide and yet produce perfect copies of itself, and that the order of the bases along the molecule could contain the genetic information.

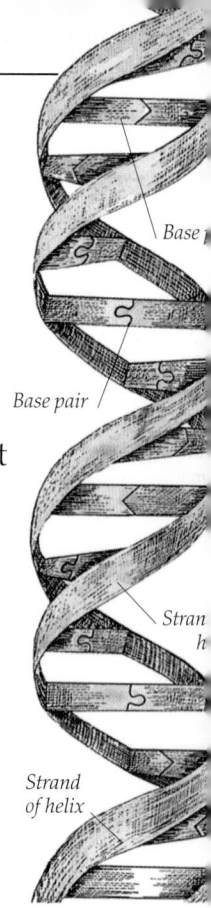

DOUBLE HELIX
This illustration show the different base pa that make up the rungs of the DNA molecule. Each base will only fit with one other base.

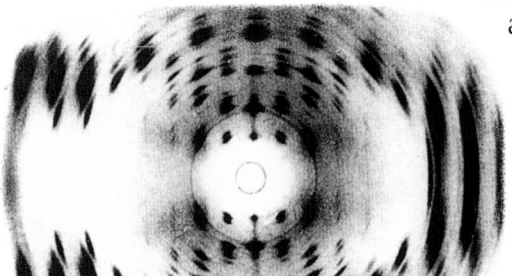

MAPPING MOLECULES
Rosalind Franklin's X-ray diffraction pictures also revealed that the sugar and phosphate units of DNA were on the outside of the helix. This was vital information for Watson and Crick.

STRANDS OF LIFE
In order to copy itself, the DNA molecule divides. The two strands of the helix come apart, little by little, as the base pairs separate. Then new bases pair on to the existing ones on each strand. The fact that each base can only pair with one other base ensures that each half of the original helix becomes an exact copy of the complete original. This is how the hereditary information is passed on from one generation to the next. Occasionally, however, a mistake can occur in the copying, and this results in a genetic mutation (p. 32). Mutations can provide a valuable source of raw material for evolution.

WINNING MODEL *(left)*
This is part of the original model of the DNA molecule, made by James Watson (left) and Francis Crick (right) in 1953. The base pairs, or rungs, are arranged along the strands of the DNA molecule in what seems like a random order. In fact, the order of the bases is full of information and can be translated according to the "genetic code."

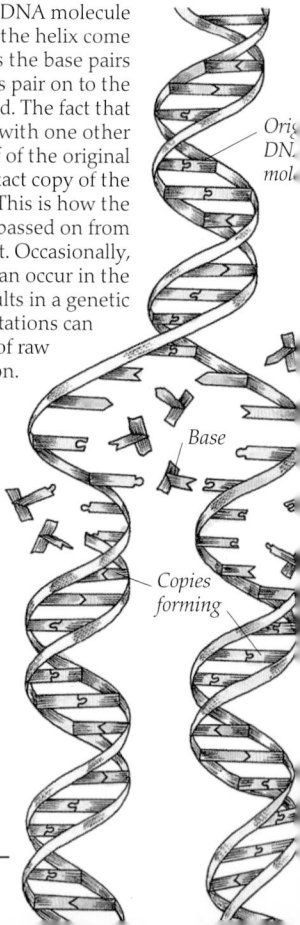

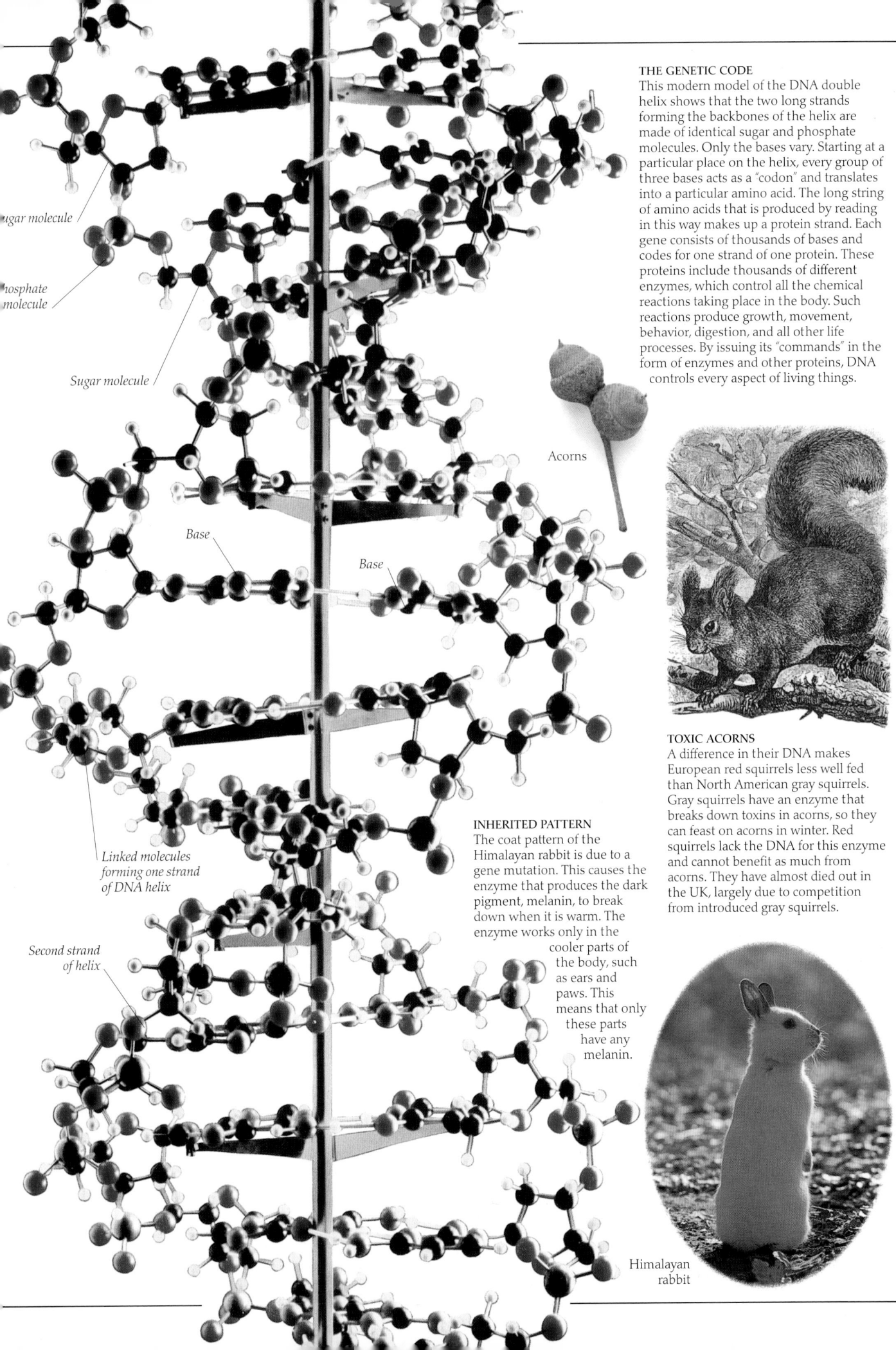

THE GENETIC CODE
This modern model of the DNA double helix shows that the two long strands forming the backbones of the helix are made of identical sugar and phosphate molecules. Only the bases vary. Starting at a particular place on the helix, every group of three bases acts as a "codon" and translates into a particular amino acid. The long string of amino acids that is produced by reading in this way makes up a protein strand. Each gene consists of thousands of bases and codes for one strand of one protein. These proteins include thousands of different enzymes, which control all the chemical reactions taking place in the body. Such reactions produce growth, movement, behavior, digestion, and all other life processes. By issuing its "commands" in the form of enzymes and other proteins, DNA controls every aspect of living things.

TOXIC ACORNS
A difference in their DNA makes European red squirrels less well fed than North American gray squirrels. Gray squirrels have an enzyme that breaks down toxins in acorns, so they can feast on acorns in winter. Red squirrels lack the DNA for this enzyme and cannot benefit as much from acorns. They have almost died out in the UK, largely due to competition from introduced gray squirrels.

INHERITED PATTERN
The coat pattern of the Himalayan rabbit is due to a gene mutation. This causes the enzyme that produces the dark pigment, melanin, to break down when it is warm. The enzyme works only in the cooler parts of the body, such as ears and paws. This means that only these parts have any melanin.

Molecular evidence

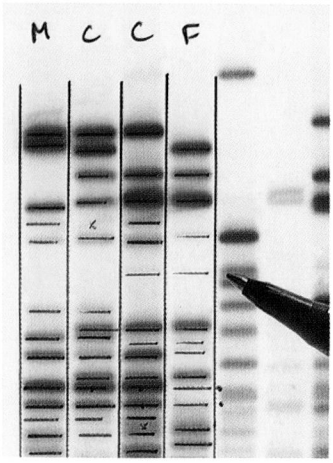

DNA FINGERPRINTS
Comparing DNA is a useful way of finding out how closely living things are related. Here DNA from two children (C and C) is being compared with DNA from each of their parents (M and F). This version of the method is called "DNA fingerprinting." It can be used to identify the father of a child, for example. DNA fingerprints can also be taken from blood stains, and these are sometimes used to help in the identification of criminals.

SINCE THE WORK OF Watson and Crick (p. 52), scientists have continue to study DNA. They have found that DNA itself, and the proteins it produces, contain vital evidence about evolution. If two new species evolve from a common ancestor, their DNA, and thus their protein molecules, slowly begin to change and build up differences. The numbe of differences is proportional to the time since they separated. This discovery was made in the 1960s and a possible explanation was proposed by a Japanese scientist, Motoo Kimura. He suggested that ma mutations (p. 32) have neither good nor bad effects. He called these "neutral mutations." Such a mutation could change one of the amino ac in a protein molecule (p. 53) without affecting how the protein does its job in the body. Kimura's theory is still disputed, but the fact that mutations build up at a regular rate is not in doubt. It is as if the molecu inside the body carry a steadily ticking clock that creates a record of the past. This can be used to check the accuracy of evolutionary trees worke out from fossils or from comparisons of the structure of living things. This independent source of evidence largely confirms the evolutionary trees already worked out, indicating that scientific ideas about evolution are correct.

DEEP FROZEN
The bodies of now-extinct mammoths a sometimes found in the icy ground of Siberia. These remains still contain DNA although it is partially broken down. Th ancient DNA can be compared with that the mammoth's relative, the elephant.

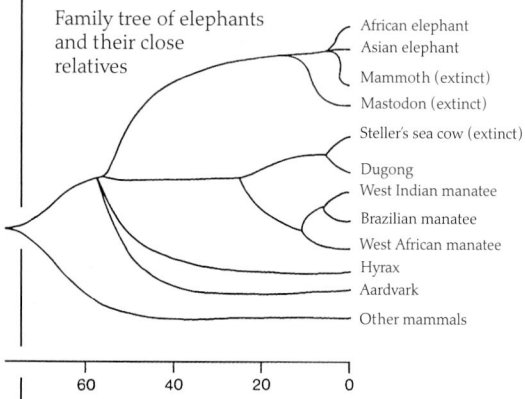

PROTEINS FROM THE PAST
One simple way of comparing proteins is to use the immune system. This is the system that animals have for defense against disease. It reacts to foreign substances very specifically, so if an animal such as a rabbit has been "vaccinated" with proteins from an elephant, its immune system will also react to proteins from a relative of the elephant, for instance a mammoth, but not as strongly. The closer the relationship, the stronger the reaction. The family tree (left) for elephants and their close relatives was worked out in this way.

Preserved mammoth from Siberia

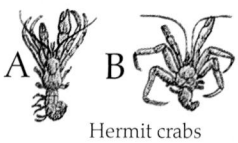

Hermit crabs

Alaskan king crab

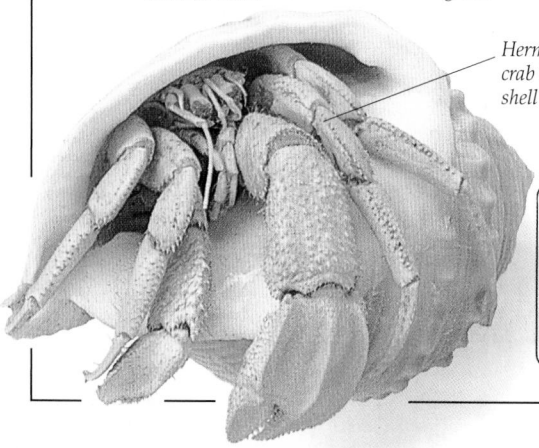

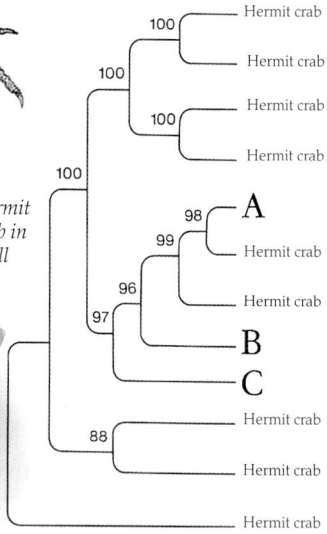

TESTING A THEORY
Hermit crabs are small and depend on the shells of mollusks for their homes. Because of their habit of living in spiral shells, the hind part of the body, the abdomen, is curved to one side. Alaskan king crabs are large and never live in mollusk shells, but zoologists suspected that they had evolved from hermit crabs because their abdomens are slightly assymmetrical, like those of hermit crabs. When DNA comparisons became possible, zoologists saw a way of testing this theory. They extracted DNA from many different species of hermit crab and from Alaskan king crabs. Comparisons showed that king crabs are indeed very closely related to the hermit crabs (left). As with the mammoths, elephants, and sea cow, the DNA confirmed what was already thought on the basis of more traditional evidence.

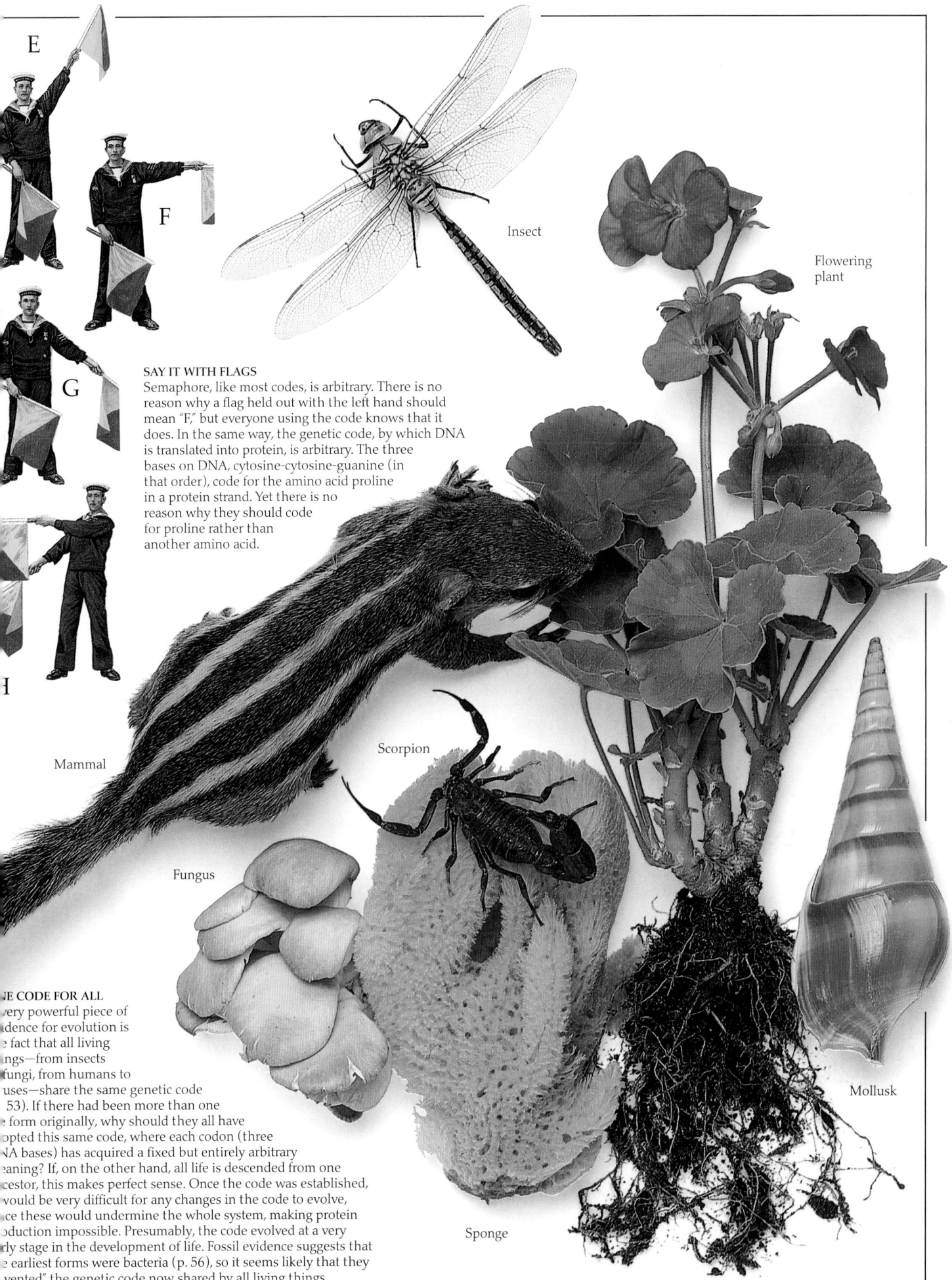

SAY IT WITH FLAGS
Semaphore, like most codes, is arbitrary. There is no reason why a flag held out with the left hand should mean "F," but everyone using the code knows that it does. In the same way, the genetic code, by which DNA is translated into protein, is arbitrary. The three bases on DNA, cytosine-cytosine-guanine (in that order), code for the amino acid proline in a protein strand. Yet there is no reason why they should code for proline rather than another amino acid.

JE CODE FOR ALL
/ery powerful piece of idence for evolution is e fact that all living ngs—from insects fungi, from humans to uses—share the same genetic code 53). If there had been more than one form originally, why should they all have opted this same code, where each codon (three NA bases) has acquired a fixed but entirely arbitrary eaning? If, on the other hand, all life is descended from one cestor, this makes perfect sense. Once the code was established, vould be very difficult for any changes in the code to evolve, ce these would undermine the whole system, making protein oduction impossible. Presumably, the code evolved at a very rly stage in the development of life. Fossil evidence suggests that e earliest forms were bacteria (p. 56), so it seems likely that they vented" the genetic code now shared by all living things.

The origin of life

ENERGY INPUT
The chemicals found in living things are far more complex than those found in rocks or sea or air. To create complex molecules from simple ones, energy is required. One likely source of this energy on early Earth was lightning.

HOW DID LIFE BEGIN? Could it have originated from nonliving matter by ordinary chemical processes? The earliest fossils are complex organ molecules 3.8 billion years old. Before that there is no solid evidence about the evolution of life, so scientists have to approach these questions in other ways. One approach is to try to re-create the conditions found on early Earth. Such experiments were first tried in t 1950s and, to most people's surprise, they readily produced the sort of complex chemicals that are found only in living things. These include the building blocks of proteins, DNA and RNA (a molecule that is similar to DNA and is involved in protein production). If complex molecules such as these could have arisen spontaneously billions of years ago, why do they not still do so today? The answer is that conditions now are very different. Most importantly, there is oxygen ir the air, whereas there was almost none in Earth's atmosphere then. Once complex chemicals had formed on early Earth, several important steps would have been required before they became genuine living things. Some scientists believe that the first major step was the formation of an RNA molecule that could make exact copies of itself. Recently, small molecules of this kind have been made in the laboratory. A second major step was the development of a relationship between RNA and proteins and the establishment of a genetic code (p. 55).

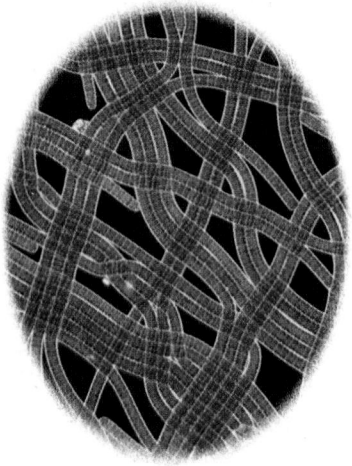

SELF-SUFFICIENCY BEGINS
The first bacteria must have lived by feeding on the complex chemicals still being produced, but in time they ate more than was being formed. When the supply ran short, many bacteria must have died out, but others, that could make their own food, evolved. These included the cyanobacteria, or blue-green algae (left).

THE OXYGEN REVOLUTION
Some bacteria use energy from the Sun to make their own food, as plants do, and in the process they release oxygen gas. When the first of these bacteria evolved, more than 3.5 billion years ago, they began to produce oxygen, which slowly built up in the air. The oxygen combined with iron in the rocks to produce bands of ironstone (right) at this time. Oxygen changed the conditions on Earth so much that many creatures became extinct. In time, oxygen in the air also allowed new, larger, and more active animals to evolve. Such active life forms would have been impossible without oxygen.

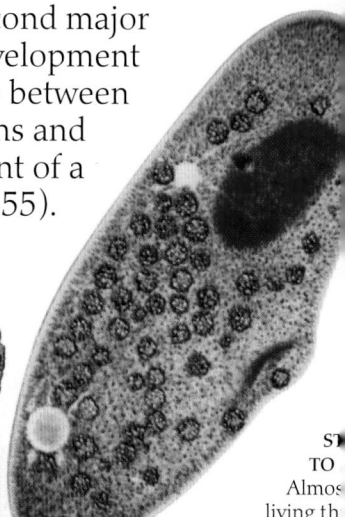

S
TO
Almos
living th
today are compose
cells. It is hard to
exactly when living th
became cellular. Some theorists sug
that the earliest life forms were "na
RNA molecules, not surrounded by
membrane. Others believe th
membrane of some sort came
before RNA. They point out that cer
large molecules spontaneously f
droplets, inside which other molec
could accumu

SEALED U
A cell is a bit like a subma
The membrane of the
acts like the hull, crea
a sealed unit in which
internal conditions ca
closely controlled. C
certain substances
allowed to pass in or

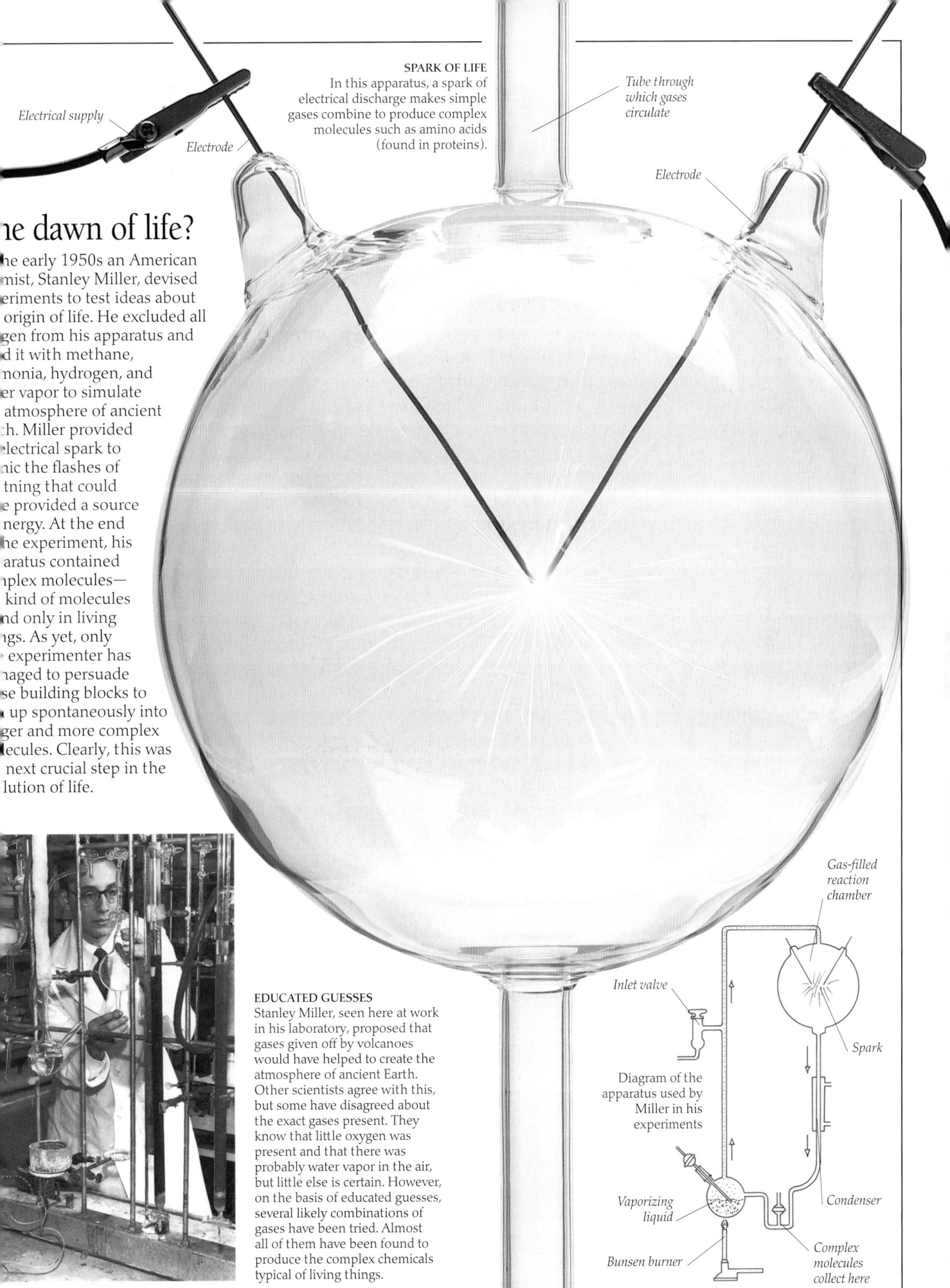

SPARK OF LIFE
In this apparatus, a spark of electrical discharge makes simple gases combine to produce complex molecules such as amino acids (found in proteins).

ne dawn of life?

he early 1950s an American mist, Stanley Miller, devised eriments to test ideas about origin of life. He excluded all gen from his apparatus and d it with methane, nonia, hydrogen, and er vapor to simulate atmosphere of ancient h. Miller provided lectrical spark to nic the flashes of tning that could e provided a source nergy. At the end he experiment, his aratus contained nplex molecules— kind of molecules nd only in living ngs. As yet, only experimenter has naged to persuade se building blocks to up spontaneously into ger and more complex lecules. Clearly, this was next crucial step in the lution of life.

EDUCATED GUESSES
Stanley Miller, seen here at work in his laboratory, proposed that gases given off by volcanoes would have helped to create the atmosphere of ancient Earth. Other scientists agree with this, but some have disagreed about the exact gases present. They know that little oxygen was present and that there was probably water vapor in the air, but little else is certain. However, on the basis of educated guesses, several likely combinations of gases have been tried. Almost all of them have been found to produce the complex chemicals typical of living things.

Diagram of the apparatus used by Miller in his experiments

Science and belief

APE OR ANGEL?
A 19th-century French cartoon shows Darwin in apelike form, bursting through the hoops of credulity and ignorance held by the French physician and philosopher Maximilien Littré (1801–1881), a supporter of Darwin. The evidence that humans arose from apelike ancestors by evolution is very strong (p. 63), but this idea troubles many people. Alfred Wallace (p. 36) solved his dilemma between science and belief by proposing that, while human beings had indeed evolved, the human spirit came from some supernatural source.

MANY DIFFERENT CULTURES have traditional beliefs about how the living world was made (p. 6). These beliefs are not usually open to question or change. Scientific ideas about the history of life are different: the details of the story are continually changing because scientists work by looking for new evidence, by questioning existing theories and trying to develop better theories. In time, some theories become well established, and their basic points are accepted as fact simply because the evidence in their favor is overwhelming. The idea that the Earth goes raound the Sun is one such theory. The idea that evolution has occurred is another. There may still be arguments over the details of how evolution occurred, but the fact that it did occur is not in doubt among scientists. One way of testing theories is to use them to make predictions and then to check those predictions. Because evolution proceeds so slowly, it is more difficult to test in this way than other scientific theories. (For the same reason, we do not normally notice evolution in action around us, even though it is continuing all the time.) Occasionally, however, evolutionary theories can be tested in the wild.
A theory about how social insects evolved was used to make a prediction about evolution in mammals, and this was later confirmed by discoveries about the naked mole rat. Theories about natural selection were tested by observing the effects of cleaner air on the peppered moth.

SCIENCE AND THE PRES
Stephen Jay Gould (1941–2002) was among the scientists who continually tested and questioned the deta of evolution theory. Sad newspapers often fail to understand this scientifi process and assume that the whole idea of evolution is in doubt. Th then report the scientific debates under dramatic and misleading headline such as the one below.

Darwin Wrong
Scientist Claims

by our Science Correspondent

CLEANER AIR, PALER MOTHS
A dark form of the peppered moth replaced the paler form in industrial areas of England from the 1850s onward. Scientists suspected that this was a result of pollution reducing the camouflage of the pale moths (p. 36). Natural selection by moth-eating birds was thought to be at work. When, in the 1970s, laws were passed to reduce pollution, an unintentional "experiment" took place, allowing scientists to check their theory about why the darker form had taken over. In the next few years the air became cleaner. As predicted, the numbers of dark moths did fall, while the paler ones increased.

ON THE WRONG TRACK?
Could scientists be totally mistaken about evolution? This claim is sometimes made by opponents of the theory. However, in science, mistaken ideas do not survive for long, because theories are tested against experimental evidence. The case of Soviet geneticist Trofim Lysenko (1898–1976) proved this point. He favored Lamarckian ideas (p. 13), since they agreed with Communist ideology, and he rose to power under Stalin. Lysenko banished Mendelian geneticists (p. 50), and dominated Soviet genetics for many years. Eventually, however, the evidence against Lamarckian inheritance was so strong that ideology had to give way to science. Lysenko was discredited and forced to resign.

Puzzle and prediction

Social insects, such as bees, wasps, and ants, live in colonies in which a single female produces all the offspring while the other members of the colony carry out duties of protection and feeding. How such social insects could have evolved has long been a puzzle. In the 1970s, the American zoologist Richard Alexander proposed an answer. He suggested that an insect species that cares for its young might evolve into a social insect as a direct result of living in a "fortress of food"—a well-defended nest to which food can be imported, or in which food is already available. He also made the bold prediction that a social mammal could evolve to live like these insects.

ASP NEST
sps are social insects, like bees d termites. Each colony builds a nplex nest, and at the center of s nest, one female can remain safe d well fed. She produces all the ung. The other wasps defend the ony or go out to collect food. en if they are killed, their nes are passed on the next generation, cause the queen shares ose genes. Until 1976, s odd way of life s known only ong insects.

Naked mole rat hills formed during tunneling

Worker gathering food

THE UNLIKELY MAMMAL
Alexander suggested that a mammal with a social life like a bee could have evolved. He predicted that if it did so, it would probably live in a place with a long dry season, where some plants have huge tubers. The mammal would be a burrower that could build its underground colony—its "fortress of food"—around these tubers. Several years later, to the amazement of scientists, South African zoologist Jennifer Jarvis revealed that the naked mole rat, an East African mammal, lives precisely as Richard Alexander had predicted.

GGING BLINDLY
ke a worker wasp, the ked mole rat worker ends its time defending the ony, bringing food to the ung, or tunneling through e ground to find the tubers on ich the colony feeds. While gging, it can close its mouth hind its front teeth, to keep from allowing soil. It is almost nd, rarely venturing to daylight.

Naked mole rat queen in burrow

Baby naked mole rats suckle at the queen's teats

UNDERGROUND QUEEN
The queen is the only mole rat in the colony to produce offspring. She keeps the other females infertile by her dominant behavior. She remains in the safety of the deepest part of the burrow (above) and is vigorously protected by the workers. In the nest chamber she suckles the young (right) until they are old enough to be fed on tubers by the workers.

SPOSABLE WORKER
e workers live and e without producing y young. When the lony is under attack a snake, workers ay sacrifice their own es in order to defend e colony, just as orker bees do.

Naked mole rat worker

The queen is larger than the workers

History of life

THE SCIENTIFIC STUDY of rocks, fossils, and living things can be used to build up a picture of what happened in the past. Hundreds of scientists, working in different parts of the world, have helped to build up this picture. The details change as new evidence is constantly being found, and there are differences of opinion among scientists about some of the specific points. However, there is broad agreement on the major events, the general course of evolution, and the time-scale.

BEFORE LIFE
Meteorites were formed at the same time as Earth (p. 29). Earth's crust solidified 4.5 billion years ago, but for millions of years Earth was empty of life. Although the early steps in the origin of life can only be guessed at (p. 56), the first fossils of bacteria are some 3.5 billion years old.

BACTERIAL FOSSILS
Bacteria evolved into many types with different ways of obtaining their food. Some cyanobacteria (p. 56) form colonies that are large enough to be seen without the aid of a microscope.

GETTING LARGER
Only at the end of the Precambrian do readily visible, larger life forms appear. Most belong to the Ediacaran fauna (p. 47).

CAMBRIAN EXPLOSION
In the early Cambrian, many different kinds of complex marine animals suddenly appear in the fossil record.

BURGESS SHALE
Cambrian rocks reveal many different groups of invertebrate animals.

PLATE MOVEMENT
Over geological time, the movement of crustal plates has caused oceans to open and close and carried continents over Earth's surface.

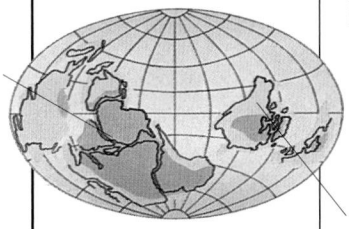

SIMPLE SURVIVORS
In this fossil colony of bryozoans, each opening contained a single tiny animal. Still found today, bryozoans have shown little change for millions of years, like many other simple creatures.

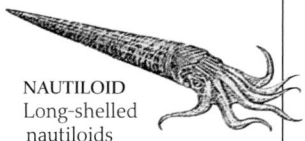

NAUTILOID
Long-shelled nautiloids such as *Orthoceras* (p. 27) were among the invertebrate animals that inhabited the seas of the early Paleozoic era.

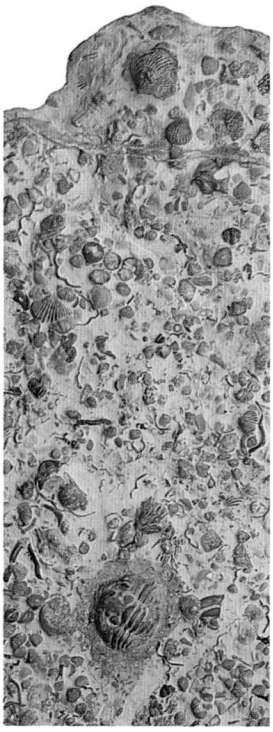

SILURIAN SEAS
Primitive arthropods known as trilobites were abundant and widespread during the Ordovician and Silurian periods. Fossils of feeding tracks show that they lived on the seafloor. They later became extinct, as did the giant sea scorpions, large armored animals up to 6 ft (2 m) long, with huge pincers.

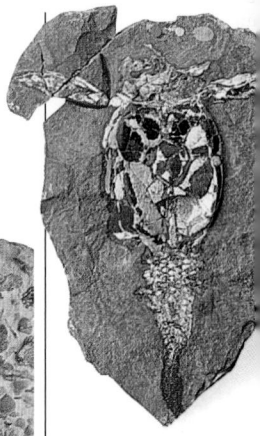

ARMORED FISH
Many of the early jawless fish were covered in plates of bony armor, probably as a defens against the giant sea scorpions..

AGE OF FISH
During Devonian times some land masses were joined together to form larg continents with vast dry regions and larg rivers and lakes. Wit seasonal and dry climates, many wate were prone to dry ou These conditions favored the survival groups of fish that could breathe air an use their muscular fi and limbs to move from one body of water to another.

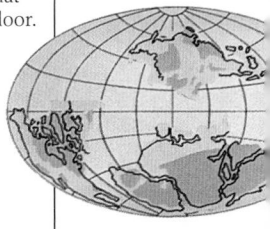

PRECAMBRIAN	CAMBRIAN PERIOD	ORDOVICIAN PERIOD	SILURIAN PERIOD	DEVONIAN PERIOD
	PALEOZOIC ERA			

ME SPAN
st of the history of life aken up by simple gle-celled animals, gely bacteria. They re the only living ngs for almost 3 billion rs. Compared with s, the extinction of the osaurs at the end of Mesozoic, 65 million rs ago, seems like a ly recent event, as es the emergence modern humans, just 0,000 years ago.

Geological time scale

MESOZOIC
PALEOZOIC
PRECAMBRIAN
3.5 BYA
2 BYA
4.5 BILLION YEARS AGO (BYA)
Bacteria first appear
Oxygen builds up in atmosphere
First fossils of multicellular animals
CENOZOIC

SSIL FERN
nts, like animals, evolved m bacterial ancestors, obably during the late cambrian. The simplest nts were one-celled algae. m these evolved weeds, mosses, ferns, es, and all other plants, st and present.

E ON LAND
fe existed in the sea til late Ordovician nes, when primitive nd plants such as lichens d mosses evolved. The first e land plants evolved in urian times, becoming e-sized in late Devonian d Carboniferous times.

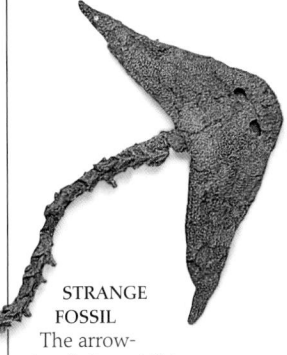

STRANGE FOSSIL
The arrow-headed amphibian *Diplocaulus* lived during the Permian. The legs of this fossil are missing.

SUPERCONTINENT
At the end of the Permian, more than 90 percent of all species died out, the largest mass extinction (p. 46) of all time. During the Permian, all the continents collided to form one supercontinent, called Pangea.

Procynosuchus, a synapsid tetrapod (p. 26) from the late Permian

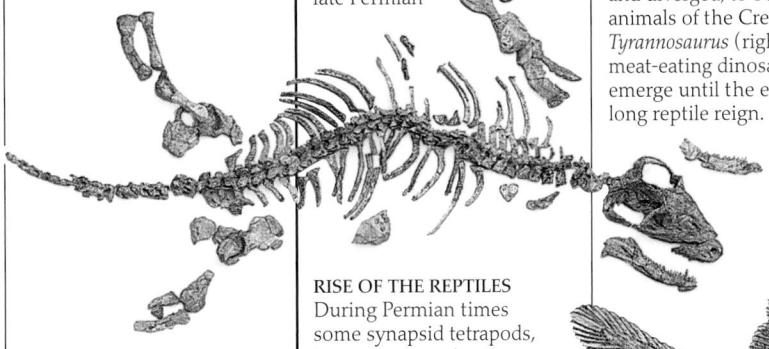

RISE OF THE REPTILES
During Permian times some synapsid tetrapods, known as cynodonts, evolved mammal-like features and became widespread and abundant. Many died out at the end of the Permian, along with many other tetrapods. This cleared the way for a new phase of reptile evolution. New synapsid groups appeared and flourished during the Triassic, along with the ancestors of dinosaurs.

SPIRAL SURVIVORS
By the Triassic, most nautiloids had tightly coiled shells. The more specialized ammonites became extinct at the end of the Cretaceous, but some nautiloids survived.

AGE OF REPTILES
During the Jurassic, the dinosaurs expanded and diverged, to become the dominant land animals of the Cretaceous period. *Tyrannosaurus* (right), a large meat-eating dinosaur, did not emerge until the end of this long reptile reign.

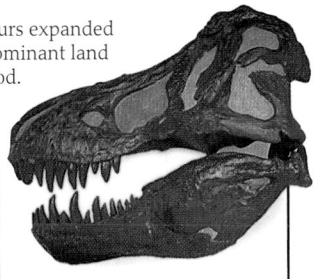

EARLY BIRD
The fossil remains of *Archaeopteryx* suggest that birds had begun to evolve from dinosaurs during the Jurassic.

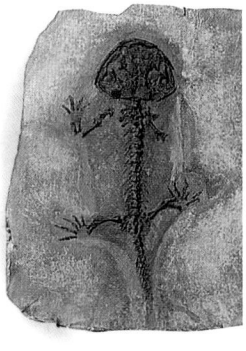

FOSSIL FROG
Recent discoveries show that modern amphibians such as salamanders and frogs originated in the Permian era, and caecilian (wormlike) amphibians in Carboniferous times.

VEGETARIAN DINOSAUR
Iguanodon (below), a plant-eating dinosaur, was common in the mid-Cretaceous but then died out. Throughout this period, many new species of dinosaur evolved, but all had died out by the end of it.

CHANGING WORLD
By the end of the Cretaceous, the single supercontinent had split up, and the continents were moving apart toward their present positions. At the end of this era there was a mass extinction in which all the dinosaurs and many other animal species died out.

CARBONIFEROUS PERIOD	PERMIAN PERIOD	TRIASSIC PERIOD	JURASSIC PERIOD	CRETACEOUS PERIOD
PALEOZOIC ERA		MESOZOIC ERA		

Up to the present

FOR THE PAST 65 MILLION YEARS, mammals have been the dominant land animals. Their ancestors were small nocturnal creatures that evolved 200 million years ago from the synapsid tetrapods (p. 26). During the age of dinosaurs, they remained small but began to diversify with aquatic and gliding forms. Some preyed upon small dinosaurs. After the dinosaurs' extinction, mammals evolved rapidly, growing larger and more diverse. So too did the birds, but their bones are fragile, so there are relatively few in the fossil record.

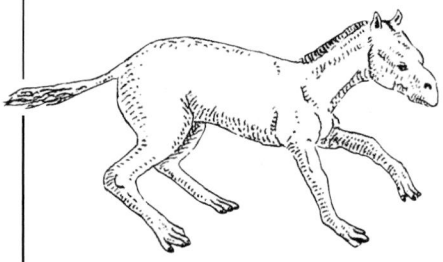

EARLY HORSE
Hyracotherium is one of the earliest horse-like mammals from 55 million years ago. The fact that evolution is not a steady march of progress is well illustrated by the horse (p. 48) and by mammal evolution in general. There has, however, been an increase in speed, intelligence, or size, in some mammal lines.

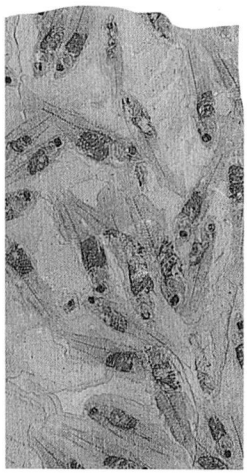

MIGHTY MASTODON
This vertebra (below) is from a mastodon (p. 14), an elephantlike animal that browsed on trees. The American mastodon survived into the Quaternary period and only died out about 10,000 years ago. Like many other large mammals that died out at this time, it may have fallen victim to human hunters.

SEAL FORERUNNER
Many of the early mammals were a bit like dogs in shape and build. They gradually evolved into more specialized forms, such as seals, deer, and horses.

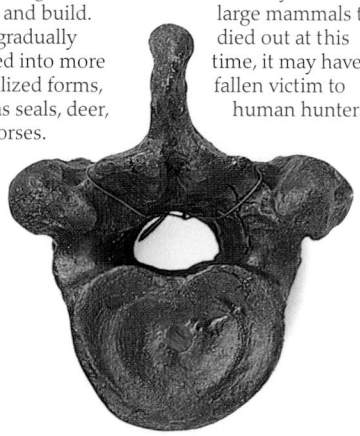

FISH AND PLANTS
It is not only the dominant animals (such as mammals) that continue to evolve, although this is the part of the story that attracts most interest. During the Cenozoic, there has been change among fish (above) and plants (left), as well as other living things.

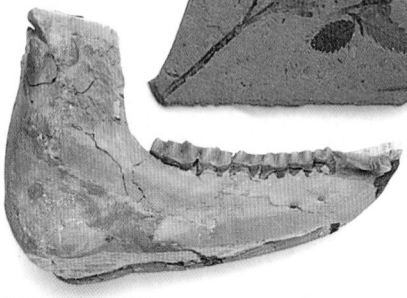

END OF THE LINE
The extinct *Palaeotherium* is known from this jaw and other fossils. It was a tapirlike animal.

ALMOST AN ELEPHANT
The fossil known as *Phiomia* is part of the group that later gave rise to elephants, mammoths, and mastodons.

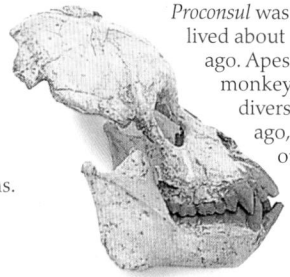

ANCIENT APE
Proconsul was an early ape that lived about 20 million years ago. Apes evolved from monkeys. They were very diverse 20 million years ago, but many died out as Earth's climate grew drier and the forests shrank.

EVOLUTIONARY ISLANDS
The separation of the continents affected mammal evolution greatly, with distinctive groups developing in isolated continents.

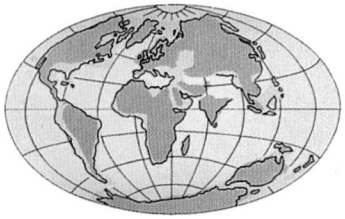

SABER TOOTH
Large tigerlike predators with massive stabbing teeth evolved to prey on slow-moving, thick-skinned creatures such as mammoths.

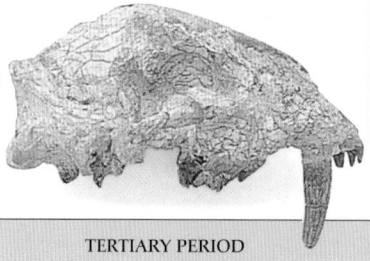

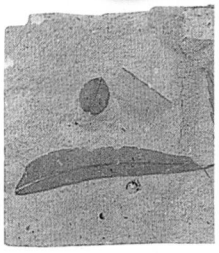

Fossil Miocene leaves

ADVANCED LEAF
These leaves, which are about 20 million years old, are from a flowering plant, the most recent plant form to evolve. These only appeared during the Cretaceous. Until then the dominant plants were the conifers and cycads.

ICE AGE BEAR
This cave bear skull is about 20,000 years old. These large bears lived during the last Ice Age and survived the extreme cold of winter by hibernating in caves. Mammals from the Quaternary period were more like present-day mammals than were those of the Tertiary, but many were far larger than their modern relatives.

VANISHED BIRD
Moas, the giant birds of New Zealand (p. 25), show what might have happened in a world without mammals—birds could have become dominant. Early in the Tertiary period, when mammals were still all fairly small, birds did, in fact, dominate. Huge flightless predatory birds evolved and preyed on mammals.

TERTIARY PERIOD

CENOZOIC ERA

Artist's impression of *Glyptodon*

ARMORED ANIMAL
The *glyptodon*, one of South America's many unique mammal species, is now extinct. After a long interval as an island, South America was reunited with North America by a fall in sea level. Competition, or predation, by invaders from the north forced many South American mammals into extinction.

Bony plates of *Glyptodon*

CLEVER NEANDERTHALS
The skull of Neanderthals suggests a brain at least as large as that of modern humans. The image of Neanderthals as dim and brutish is based on a mistaken 19th-century study of a skeleton. However, they were very strong and stocky and seem to have been well suited to the Ice Age climate.

MODERN WORLD
he Quaternary, the continents almost reached their present itions. Their slow movement ut the globe is still continuing, vever, and this produces hquakes in some places, such as ifornia. Ice ages and dly fluctuating ates have been an ortant factor in lution during the aternary period, cooling climate all over the world.

LEAF EATER
Megatherium, the giant ground sloth of South America, probably fed by sitting on its haunches and pulling down tree branches or whole trees to eat the leaves.

QUATERNARY PERIOD

CENOZOIC ERA

Human evolution

The fossil record gives a clear picture of how upright-walking, large-brained creatures called hominids evolved from an apelike ancestor. Fossil remains have been found of some 20 human-related species that have lived and died out over the last 6 million years since humans and chimps diverged. Few are represented by complete skeletons but they do indicate that small apelike human relatives walked upright at least 4 million years ago before there was any significant increase in brain size, which happened around 2.5 million years ago. The first members of our species (*Homo sapiens*) appeared in Africa some 200,000 years ago.

Skull of *Homo erectus*

Flint hand ax from 200,000 years ago

MAKING TOOLS
Fossil skulls, like this one of *Homo erectus*, show that the human brain gradually grew larger, beginning about 2.5 million years ago. At the same time, the ridges above the eyes became smaller, and the face and jaw began to jut out less. Increasing intelligence and the ability to make better tools apparently went together. The earliest stone tools, made in Africa about 2.5 million years ago, were simpler than the hand ax shown here.

Modern human skull

BIGGER BRAINS
Increasing intelligence undoubtedly contributed to the survival of early hominids. For example, *Homo erectus* cooperated to hunt large animals, and this would have required speech and intelligence. But the very great intelligence and creativity of modern humans seem to go beyond what might have aided survival in the wild. It is difficult to see musical gifts or mathematical abilities as a result of natural selection. Some human behavior, good and bad, actually runs contrary to natural selection.

Mozart, the musical child prodigy

Classifying life

TAXONOMY—THE SCIENCE OF CLASSIFYING ORGANISMS, both living and fossil—began with the work of Carl Linnaeus in the 18th century. Linnaeus set up a hierarchy of categories for grouping organisms with similar physical characteristics. Cladistics, or phylogenetics, is an alternative system developed in the 1950s and 1960s. It uses genetics, as well as physical characteristics, to sort organisms into groups called clades. From these, "family trees" are constructed to show the evolutionary development of species and the relationships between them.

CARL LINNAEUS
Linnaeus (1707–1778) was a Swedish botanist who studied and lectured at Uppsala University. Often referred to as the "father of taxonomy," he spent much of his life collecting, classifying, and naming plants and animals. In 1735, Linnaeus published the first edition of *Systema Naturae*, his classification of living organisms. Linnaeus's system—and his method of naming organisms—remains in use today.

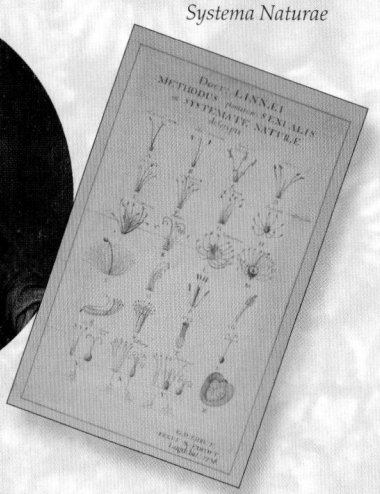

Illustration from *Systema Naturae*

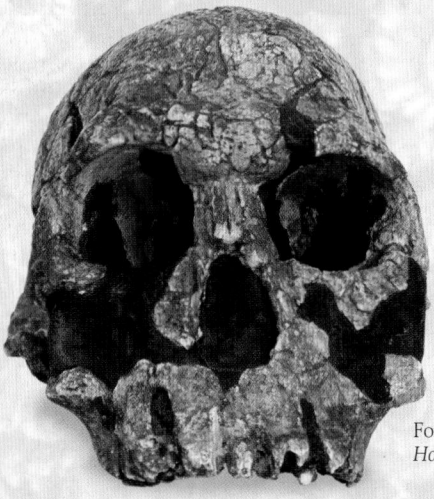

Fossil skull of *Homo habilis*

NAMING ORGANISMS
Linnaeus adopted Latin as the language of taxonomy. He gave each species a unique two-word name, or binomial, by combining its Latin genus and species names. For example, *Homo sapiens* is the binomial for modern humans. What makes the name unique is the species part. Extinct humans also carry the generic name *Homo*, such as *Homo habilis* ("handy man"), but only modern humans are referred to as *Homo sapiens* ("knowing man").

WHAT IS A SPECIES?
The basic unit of classification is the species. This is defined as a group of similar individuals that are capable of breeding together in the wild to produce fertile offspring (as opposed to infertile hybrids). For example, the Indian rhinoceros (*Rhinoceros unicornis*) cannot breed successfuly with any other of the five rhinoceros species, including the Javan rhinoceros (*Rhinoceros sondaicus*), the other one-horned species.

Indian rhinoceroses

LINNAEAN CLASSIFICATION
The kingdom, the largest grouping, is at the top of Linnaeus's classification hierarchy. There are five kingdoms, which separate livin things into plants, fungi, animals, bacteria, an proctoctists. Each kingdom is divided into eve smaller categories. The smaller the category, the fewer the organisms in it and the more features they have in common. At the bottor of the hierarchy is the species—the most exclusive unit of classification, containing ju one organism. The chart below shows the classification of the Indian rhinoceros.

KINGDOM: ANIMALIA
(Animals: 35 phyla).
The kingdom Animalia contains organisms th take food into their bodies and that develop from embryos.

PHYLUM: CHORDATA
(Chordates: 12 classes)
All animals in this phylum have a notocord—a precursor of the backbone—at some point in their lives.

CLASS: MAMMALIA
(Mammals: 28 orders)
Grouped in the class Mammalia are all animal that possess a single jawbone, fur, and mammary (milk-producing) glands.

ORDER: PERISSODACTYLA
(Odd-toed hoofed mammals: 3 families)
This is a group of plant-eating mammals that walk on odd-numbered toes. It includes horses, zebras, tapirs, and rhinoceroses.

FAMILY: RHINOCEROTIDAE
(Rhinoceroses: 5 genera)
This family within the Perissodactyla order contains the rhinoceroses—odd-toed hoofed mammals with horns on their noses.

GENUS: *RHINOCEROS*
(One-horned rhinoceroses: 2 species)
The genus *Rhinoceros* is made up of the one-horned rhinoceroses—the Indian and Javan rhinoceroses.

SPECIES: *UNICORNIS*
(Indian rhinoceros)
Found in Nepal, Bhutan, and India, this rhinoceros cannot breed with the smaller Javar rhinoceros, the other member of its genus.

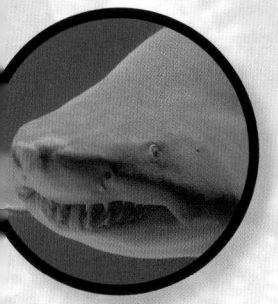

Sharks

Amphibians

Crocodiles

In cladistics, groupings work differently from those used in Linnaean classification, which is why crocodiles but not other reptiles are shown in this diagram

Birds

Mammals

Ray-finned fish

Crocodiles are featherless

Flight feathers—feathers that are adapted for flight (dinosaurs had nonflight feathers)

Mammals have one pair of holes behind the eyes

Postorbital skull openings—two pairs of holes in the skull behind the eye

Amphibians branch off, since their eggs are not waterproof

Amniotic egg—a waterproof membrane around a developing embryo

These fish have fins made of spines and skin, rather than muscular limbs

Four limbs—muscular limbs characterize the tetrapods

Sharks branch off, since their vertebral column is made of cartilage, not bone

Bony skeleton—vertebral column and other parts of skeleton made of bone

Common ancestor

Vertebral column—a jointed and flexible rod of bone or cartilage from head to tail

ILLI HENNIG
ladistics was founded by the erman biologist Willi Hennig (913–1976). An expert on flies and osquitoes, Hennig published his ost influential work, *A Basic utline of a Theory of Phylogenetic ystematics*, in 1950.

CLADISTICS FAMILY TREE

The diagram above shows a group of organisms descended from a common ancestor. This type diagram is known as a cladogram, or phylogeny. The animals in the diagram are part of the chordate clade—the vertebrates. They are all related to the first vertebrate, which appeared around 540 million years ago. The branching patterns are the result of evolution. Each new characteristic that evolves over time, indicated by a black dot, produces a point of divergence. The animal group that does not possess this characteristic branches off the main trunk of the diagram.

Cladograms and the fossil record

Thanks to the fossil record, which tells us about the characteristics of extinct organisms, cladograms can be used to show the relationships between living and extinct groups. Here, the mammal line of the main diagram has been amended to include two extinct groups of mammal-like reptiles—dicynodonts and pelycosaurs. Like mammals, they developed in an amniotic egg and had a skull opening behind each eye (in humans this is reduced to an indentation). The development of hair separates the mammals from the dicynodonts and the pelycosaurs.

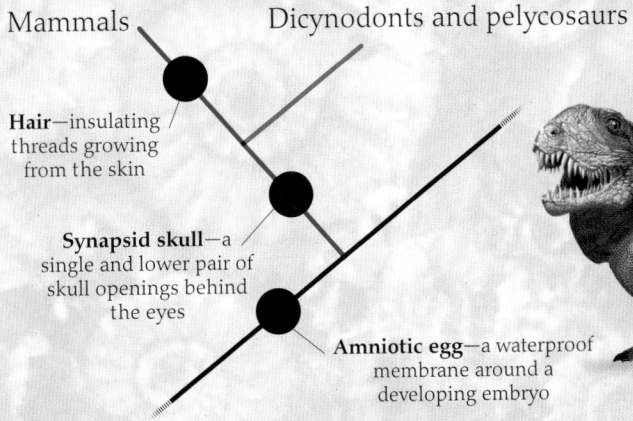

Dimetrodon, an extinct pelycosaur

Discoveries in evolution

OUR UNDERSTANDING OF LIFE AND ITS HISTORY has developed since Classical times, when scholars first questioned the nature of plants and animals and their fossil remains. Hundreds of years of discoveries, especially those of the 19th and 20th centuries, increased our knowledge of the abundance, diversity, complexity, and evolution of life. Today, we understand the connections between the molecular and genetic makeup of a single cell and the whole of life and its evolution over 3.5 billion years.

c. 350–340 BCE
Aristotle, the ancient Greek naturalist, closely observes nature. He identifies around 560 different types of animal.

322 BCE
In Greece, Theophrastus, Aristotle's pupil, publishes *Historia Plantarum*, which classifies nearly 500 types of plant, and *De Causis Plantarum*, which explains plant growth.

c. 200 CE
Early Christian philosopher Tertullian asserts that fossils found on mountains were deposited there by the waters of the biblical flood. This idea is known as diluvialism.

1551
Conrad Gesner, a Swiss physician and naturalist, publishes *Historia Animalium*, a catalog of the then known animals. He follows this in 1565 with *De Rerum Fossilium* ("On Things Dug Out of the Earth"), which is one of the first illustrated catalogs of fossils.

1673
Antoni van Leeuwenhoek, a Dutch draper and amateur naturalist, uses a microscope to reveal details of animal and plant cells for the first time. His microscope can magnify objects 250 times.

1694
Rudolph Jakob Camerarius, a German professor of physics at the University of Tubingen, publishes his *Epistola de Sexu Plantarium*. He includes experimental evidence to show that plants reproduce sexually with the deposit of male pollen on the female stigma.

Hibiscus rosa-sinensis flower, showing a long stigma

Statue of Aristotle

1753
Swedish naturalist and botanist Carl Linnaeus publishes *Species Plantarum*, which forms the basis of the modern classification of plants.

1758
Carl Linnaeus's book *Systema Naturae* forms the basis of the modern classification of animals. Modern humans are formally classified as *Homo sapiens* for the first time.

1796
Georges Cuvier, a French naturalist and anatomist, analyzes the skeletal structure of the extinct *Megatherium* from an illustration and concludes that it had been a giant ground sloth. Cuvier's work shows how all vertebrates have a common basic skeletal structure, whose modifications give clues to how each animal lives.

Fossilized claw of *Megatherium*

1801
American showman Charles Wilson Peale excavates the skeleton of a mastodon, an extinct relative of the elephant.

1802
English clergyman William Paley publishes *Natural Theology, or Evidence of the Existence and Attributes of the Deity*, which views all adaptation in the natural world as evidence of God's handiwork.

1809
The publication of a treatise *Philosophie Zoologie* by French naturalist Jean-Baptiste de Lamarck, gives the first reasoned theory of "transformism," which we now know as evolution.

1822
British doctor and fossil hunter Gideon Mant discovers teeth from an extinct giant reptile t he names *Iguanodon*.

1826
German biologist Karl Ernst von Baer discove the egg cells in female mammals. This lays th foundation of modern embryology, describin embryonic development from egg stage to bir

1830–1833
Charles Lyell, a British geologist, publishes hi *Principles of Geology*, which argues that the distant past should be explored only through understanding of the natural forces operating the present. This becomes known as the principle of uniformitarianism.

1832–1836
HMS *Beagle* makes a round-the-world survey voyage under Captain Robert Fitzroy, with English naturalist Charles Darwin invited as the expedition's naturalist.

1837
Charles Darwin begins a notebook on the "transmutation" of species.

19th-century dinosaur illustration

1841
British anatomist Richard Owen coins the name dinosaur ("terrible lizard") and publishes the first description of the dinosaurs' defining characteristics.

1844
The anonymously published book *Vestiges of the Natural History of Creation* outlines a theor for the evolution of life from primitive single-celled organisms to more complex, advanced forms such as humans. In 1884, it is finally revealed that the book was written by the Scottish publisher Robert Chambers.

1844
Charles Darwin shows an outline of his theory of evolution to the British botanist Joseph Hooker.

1854
Alfred Wallace, a British naturalist and professional collector, independently comes up with the idea of evolution by natural selection while working in Malaysia and Indonesia.

1858
Charles Darwin and Alfred Wallace produce a short joint paper on evolution by natural selection. Its publication is arranged by Joseph Hooker and Charles Lyell.

1859
Charles Darwin publishes his book *On the Origin of Species*, which outlines his ideas on evolution

)
sh biologist Thomas Henry Huxley defends vin's theory of evolution at the Oxford ting of the British Association for the ancement of Science, when it is attacked by Bishop of Oxford, Samuel Wilberforce.

Model of *Archaeopteryx*

-1
Germany, a fossil of *Archaeopteryx*, a primitive l, is found. It has impressions of feathers and ng, bony tail. Huxley realizes that this fossil s birds and reptiles, making it the first good dence to support Darwin's theory of evolution.

-3
first extinct human relative (*Homo nderthalensis*) is described and named by liam King, a geology professor in Galway, and. The fossil remains had been found in rmany in 1856, but were not at first thought be different from modern humans.

-6
strian monk Gregor Mendel publishes an ount of his experiments with breeding plants. He realizes that peas carry "particles" heredity (now called genes), some of which more dominant than others.

56
tish physicist William Thomson, later Lord lvin, says that Earth is 100 million years old most—not the many hundreds of millions of rs suggested by Darwin and Lyell. In fact, th is about 4.5 billion years old—closer to rwin and Lyell's estimate than Thomson's.

70s
st Haeckel, a German biologist and turalist, develops the idea of "evolution as ogress," which assumes that all nature is oving toward a final goal: human beings.

07
nerican geneticist Thomas Hunt Morgan gins his work on fruit flies. His research ll help to show that most characteristics are ntrolled by many genes (tiny stretches of e molecule DNA).

1930
English mathematician Ronald Fisher publishes *The Genetical Theory of Natural Selection*. It proves that Mendel's ideas on genetics support Darwin's theory of natural selection, rather than oppose it, as was previously thought.

1953
The double-helix structure of the DNA molecule is published by American James Watson and Englishman Francis Crick.

1962
American scientists Linus Pauling and Emile Zuckerkandl develop the idea of the molecular clock. This uses differences in DNA sequences and proteins between species to calculate how long ago two species diverged.

1968
American geneticist Sewell Wright publishes the first volume of his treatise on *Evolution and the Genetics of Populations*. He uses mathematics to link genetics to natural selection, and develops the idea of genetic drift—that random changes can occur in genes by chance, rather than by natural selection.

1968
Japanese geneticist Motoo Kimura proposes his neutral theory of molecular evolution, which states that genetic changes can occur at the molecular level that have no influence on an individual's fitness.

Dolly the cloned sheep, 1996

1996
British biologists Ian Wilmut and Keith Campbell clone (reproduce) a lamb called Dolly from a single adult udder cell of a black-faced ewe. Dolly is an exact genetic copy of that ewe, instead of having inherited her genes from two genetically different parents. Scientists think that cloning can help genetic research, but some people see it as tampering with nature.

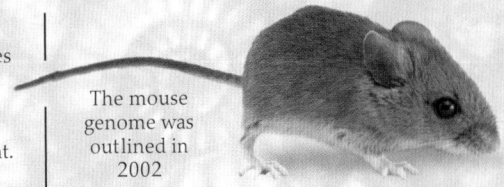

The mouse genome was outlined in 2002

2000
The working draft of the international Human Genome Project is published. The project aims to find the makeup of the human genome—the sequence of base pairs that make up human DNA and the 25,000 or so human genes. The project began in 1990, headed by James Watson.

2002
The mouse genome is outlined. Of the mouse's 30,000 or so genes, some 80 percent have direct counterparts in the human genome, and 99 percent show some similarity.

2003
The complete draft of the human genome is published. Further analysis continues.

2005
Publication of the outline of chimp genome, which is only 2.7 percent different from the human genome. These differences, which include certain genes involved in speech development, have evolved over the 6 million years or so since humans and chimps last shared a common ancestor.

2006
The Neanderthal Genome Project is announced by Germany's Max Planck Institute. It is already known that Neanderthal and human DNA is 99.5 percent identical, and that the genomes are roughly the same size. Ancient DNA from a 38,000-year-old male Neanderthal from Croatia is currently being extracted and sequenced to produce an outline of the Neanderthal genome.

Human genome research, 1990 to present

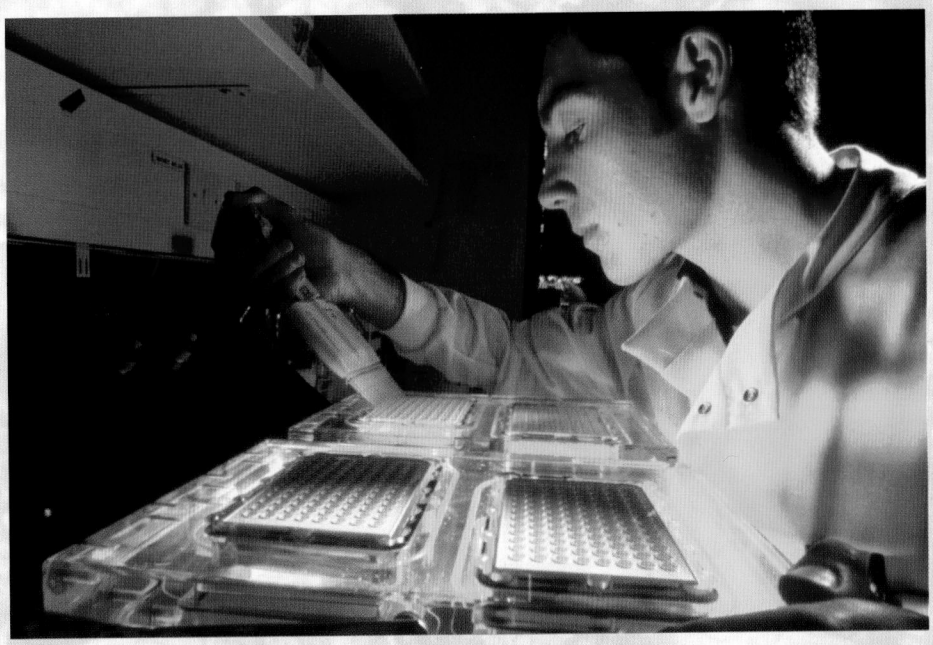

Find out more

THE SCIENTIFIC STUDY OF EVOLUTION is over 150 years old. Since Darwin and Wallace first proposed their theory in 1858, a vast amount has been published by scientists on the subject. Never before has there been so much information available about evolution and related topics such as fossils, natural history, and the protection and conservation of wildlife. You can find facts, figures, and stories in public libraries and on the internet, get a feel for the stunning variety of animal life at a zoo, and encounter the creatures of the past in a museum. You can also get involved by joining a conservation group or taking up a nature hobby.

Field Museum, Chicago, Illinois

Meeting the animals at Singapore Zoo

ZOOS AND BOTANICAL GARDENS

The world's major zoos and botanical gardens allo to appreciate life's diversity and abundance and ge close to the extraordinary animals and plants that populate our planet. Today, zoos and botanical gardens also play a vital role in the conservation o rare and endangered species, reminding us of how relate to and affect the natural world around us.

USEFUL WEBSITES

- Understanding Evolution, a website from the Museum of Paleontology, California, is an excellent in-depth interactive site on evolution: **http://evolution.berkeley.edu**
- The American Museum of Natural History has an outstanding natural history and evolution site; its "Ology" section is specially for kids: **www.amnh.org**
- The website of the Smithsonian Institution has an "Explore a topic" link with resources on subjects such as "The Evolving Earth" and "The Diversity of Life": **www.mnh.si.edu**
- Based on the PBS miniseries Evolution, this website is one of the most comprehensive evolutionary science sites on the internet, with FAQs, online activities, and more: **http://www.pbs.org/wqbh/evolution/**
- The first website dedicated entirely to the life and tmes of Charles Darwin features detailed maps of the Beagle voyage: **www.aboutdarwin.com**
- The World Wildlife Fund's website has databases, photo galleries, video clips, images from camera traps, games, and more: **www.wwf.org**
- The National Audubon Society's kids' section includes bird-themed games and suggestions for how you can help protect birds: **www.audubon.org/educate/kids/**
- The IUCN's Red List (see opposite) has a searchable website with information on species facing a high risk of global extinction: **www.iucnredlist.org**

VISIT A MUSEUM

A visit to a natural history museum is a great way t get a good overview of the development of life on Earth, and the weird and wonderful species that populated the planet in past ages. Many museums have interactive displays and some exhibit spectacu dinosaur skeletons. Most museums maintain their own websites that give opening times and backgro information on the objects in their collections.

URE HOBBIES
childhood, Charles Darwin was an avid collector
igs. A hands-on nature hobby, such as bird-
hing, bug hunting, or plant identification, is still
way of getting to know how nature works.
ng photos and making notes and drawings will
you learn to identify different species. If you do
ct animal specimens, make sure you return them
eir natural habitats.
plants should be
rved rather
picked.

Using a net is an easy way to catch flying insects, but they should always be released again once you have studied them

Places to visit

AMERICAN MUSEUM OF NATURAL HISTORY, NEW YORK CITY
The museum has the world's single largest collection of dinosaur fossils, with over 100 specimens on show. Pay them a visit at night, on one of the museum's sleepovers!

THE FIELD MUSEUM, CHICAGO, ILLINOIS
The Evolving Planet exhibit at this world-class museum takes visitors on a four-billion-year tour of life on Earth.

PAGE MUSEUM AT THE LA BREA TAR PITS, LOS ANGELES, CALIFORNIA
On the site of the famous tar pits, you can see the remains of many extinct animals that got stuck there.

DINOSAUR VALLEY STATE PARK, GLEN ROSE, TEXAS
In the streambed of the Paluxy River, you can take a look at some of the best-preserved dinosaur footprints in the world.

Conservation work on a reed bed

Drawer with fossil specimens

COLLECTING FOSSILS
Fossils provide important and fascinating evidence for evolution. Fossil collecting is a hobby that can be enjoyed by anyone, but it is essential to check whether it is legal to collect from a particular site, since many countries have strict rules about collecting and you may need a license. Always make sure you are supervised by an adult when you are fossil collecting, and use the correct equipment, such as rock hammers, safety helmets, goggles, and gloves. Never collect below cliffs or anywhere there might be rockfalls.

CAL CONSERVATION GROUPS
ry region has its own natural history heritage.
ere is now a growing appreciation of how
uable, and how fragile, this heritage is. Many
aservation groups work to protect local
dlife and its habitats, and the fossil sites that
us about life in the past. Most groups
ganize days when you can take an active part
conservation by helping with tasks such as
aring scrub, replanting, and so on. Public
raries and web-based searches can provide
mes and addresses of local groups.

INTERNATIONAL CONSERVATION
Your school class could fund-raise and campaign for international organizations like the World Wildlife Fund, which promotes the cause of wildlife conservation worldwide. The International Union for the Conservation of Nature (IUCN) is a global body that works to find solutions to problems that put species at risk. Its Red List gives the current status of plant and animal species that are threatened with extinction. It is updated regularly.

Conservation workers help a cheetah in Africa

Glossary

ACQUIRED CHARACTERISTICS The noninheritable characteristics acquired by an organism in its lifetime. Large muscles produced by weight-lifting are acquired characteristics.

ADAPTATION The process of modification by natural selection that makes an organism more able to survive and reproduce in its environment. Also, any characteristic produced by this process.

ALLELE One of two or more alternative forms of the same gene.

AMINO ACID One of a group of 20 carbon-based molecules that form the building blocks of thousands of different proteins in living things.

ARTIFICIAL SELECTION The alteration of a population of plants or animals by selective breeding carried out by humans. Dog breeds, for example, are produced by artificial selection.

BASE A chemical compound that forms part of a DNA molecule. Bases form the "rungs" of the molecule's ladderlike structure, with two bases (a base pair) per rung.

BINOMIAL The two-word scientific name of an organism, made up of its Latin genus and species names. The binomial of modern humans, for example, is *Homo sapiens*.

CAMBRIAN EXPLOSION The emergence of many new and complex life forms in the Cambrian Period (542–488 million years ago).

CATASTROPHE THEORY The 19th-century idea that the change in fossils from rocks of one geological period to the next could be explained by global catastrophes such as great floods, powerful earthquakes, or changes in climate.

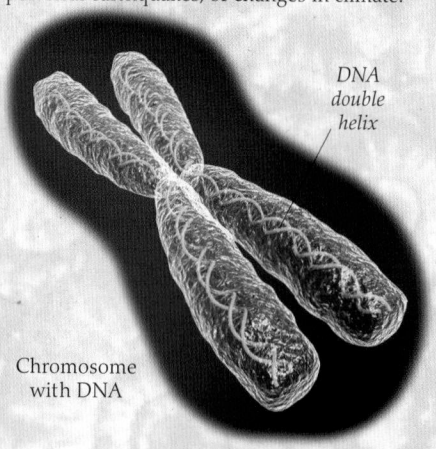

Chromosome with DNA

CELL A tiny unit of living matter. Cells are the building blocks of all living things. The control center of a cell is the nucleus.

CHROMOSOMES Threadlike DNA packages found in the cell nucleus. They carry genes and all the information needed to make a cell work.

CLADISTICS A method of classification in which members of a group, or clade, share a more recent common ancestor with one another than with members of any other group. Cladistics is also known as phylogenetics.

CLADOGRAM A branching diagram, or phylogeny, showing the evolutionary history and interrelationship of species.

CLONE To produce a genetic replica of a cell or organism; also, the replica itself. Cloning occurs in organisms that reproduce from a single parent (asexual reproduction). Scientists have succeeded in cloning organisms artificially in the laboratory.

COMMON ANCESTOR An ancestral species shared by two or more species. Modern humans and chimps share a common ancestor that lived at least six million years ago.

COMPETITION The struggle between organisms for limited resources, leading to natural selection.

DARWINISM The original theory proposed by Darwin that species evolve from other species by natural selection. Neo-Darwinism is modified by the addition of Mendelism, of which Darwin was not aware.

DILUVIALISM The mistaken idea that all rock strata and fossils were laid down at the same time by catastrophic flooding.

DINOSAURS An extinct group of land-dwelling reptiles that lived in the Mesozoic Era (251–65 million years ago).

DNA Short for deoxyribonucleic acid, which is present in every cell and which gives the hereditary characteristics to a parent organism.

DOMINANT GENE A gene (allele) that shows itself in a living organism's phenotype, or physical form. In humans, the gene for brown eyes is dominant over the gene for blue eyes.

DOUBLE HELIX The coiled, twisted ladder shape of the DNA molecule.

EMBRYO An unborn living organism at an early stage of development.

ENZYME A protein that speeds up and regulates chemical reactions.

EVOLUTION Changes in the genetics and forms of organisms over time.

EXTINCTION The natural dying out of species.

FOSSIL The preserved trace of a once-living organism. Fossils are usually bodily remains (bones, teeth, or shells), footprints, dung, or the impressions of body features.

FOSSILIZATION The way that the buried remains of organisms are preserved when th sediment around them is transformed into r

GENE A stretch of DNA that carries instruct to make a particular protein. Genes are the basic units of heredity, which are passed on to the next generation.

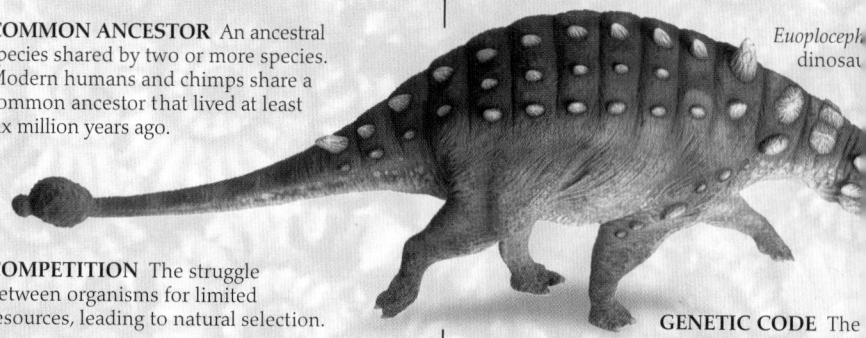

Euoplocepha dinosau

GENETIC CODE The arrangement of bases in a DNA molecule. The genetic code tells a cell h to convert the sequence of bases into a seque of amino acids, from which proteins can be ba

GENETIC DRIFT Randomly occurring char in the genetic makeup of a population, occurr at the molecular level, rather than by selecti

GENOME All the DNA in a cell or organism

GENOTYPE The genetic information that an organism inherits from its parents. The genotype interacts with the environment to produce the organism's phenotype.

GENUS A category of classification contain one or more closely related species.

GEOLOGICAL PERIOD A unit of time represented by a sequence of rock strata and their characteristic fossils. Geological periods are subdivided into epochs and stage and grouped into eras.

Fossilized frog

Mule—a hybrid of a donkey and a horse

REDITY The etic link between cessive generations ving organisms.

MINID One of a group pright-walking, large- ned mammals that evolved n apelike ancestors. mans are hominids.

BRID The offspring of a ss between two separate but ted species. Hybrids are rtile and cannot reproduce.

AGE An extremely cold iod in Earth's history when the ice ets were much larger than they are today.

HERITANCE The passing on of racteristics from generation to generation.

TERBREEDING Sexual reproduction ween organisms that involves the exchange eproductive cells and their DNA.

Invertebrate worm

TERMEDIATE A living or fossil species that resents an "in-between" stage or link in the lution of a new group from an existing one.

VERTEBRATE An animal lacking a backbone.

OLATING MECHANISM Scents, sounds, ors, and behavioral signals used by a species to ognize its own kind for breeding.

MARCKISM A mistaken theory proposed Jean-Baptiste Lamarck that an individual can erit characteristics acquired by its parents ing their lifetime.

CUS The position of particular e on a chromosome.

ASS EXTINCTION Rare, relatively ef catastrophic events that cause a nificant percentage of organisms on rth to die out.

ENDELISM The rules governing the y that individual characteristics are ssed from parent organisms to their spring via dominant, recessive, and -linked genes.

GRATION The movement of organisms m one place to another, either as individuals, ups, or whole populations. If this results in organisms becoming isolated from the t of their species, they may eventually olve into a new species.

MOLECULE A tiny particle of a chemical substance. Molecules are made up of even smaller particles called atoms.

MUTATION A change in a cell's genetic material. If a mutation occurs in a reproductive cell, it can be passed on from one generation to another.

NATURAL SELECTION The process by which organisms that are poorly suited to their environment are slowly weeded out because they fail to survive. Those that are fitter and well adapted to their environment survive better, and produce more offspring. As a result, they pass on their genes to future generations.

NATURAL THEOLOGY The idea that the adaptation of organisms to their surroundings is evidence of design by a creator God.

PHENOTYPE The physical characteristics of an organism that result from the interaction between its genotype and the environment.

PLATE TECTONICS The slow movement of the solid rocky plates of Earth's outer layer, or crust, as new seafloor rocks are generated and older seafloor rocks are recycled.

PROTEIN A chainlike molecule made up of amino acids. Proteins form the organic (carbon-based) compounds that are characteristic of living things.

RECAPITULATION The mistaken 19th-century idea that as an embryo develops it goes through all the evolutionary stages of its ancestors.

Migrating monarch butterflies

RECESSIVE GENE A gene (allele) that is hidden when it is partnered by a dominant gene. It only shows in the phenotype if it is partnered by an identical recessive gene. In humans, the gene for red hair is recessive.

RNA (Ribonucleic acid) RNA is a molecule similar to DNA. It is present in all organisms and translates the genetic code into proteins.

SEDIMENTARY ROCK A type of rock formed from the debris of other rocks and sometimes the remains of living organisms.

SEXUAL SELECTION A type of selection in which individuals are favored (selected) over others of the same sex because of their mating behavior. Examples include males fighting for access to females, and females choosing males on the basis of their courtship displays.

Courtship display in ducks

SPECIES A group of organisms that can breed together in the wild. Also a basic unit of classification, referred to by its Latin binomial.

SPONTANEOUS GENERATION The false notion that new microorganisms spontaneously arise from nonliving matter, such as wet straw.

SUBSPECIES A group within a species that has recognizable characteristics, often geographically separated from the rest of the species so that interbreeding is not possible. This is often the first step in the formation of a new species.

TAXONOMY The science of classifying and naming living and extinct organisms.

TETRAPOD An vertebrate with four limbs, or an animal that has evolved from one.

UNIFORMITARIANISM The 19th-century idea that the past can be understood only in relation to the natural forces operating in the present.

VARIATION The naturally occurring differences between individuals and populations of the same species that have a genetic basis, such as color and pattern variations on the shells of seashore mollusks.

VERTEBRATE An animal with a backbone, or spine. The individual bones of the spine are known as vertebrae.

Index

A

adaptation, 36, 38-39, 41, 49
Agassiz, Louis, 17
Agrias claudina spp., 13
Alexander, Richard, 59
algae, 61, blue-green, 26, 56
alleles, 50, 51
ammonites, 9, 26, 27, 46, 61
amphibians, 60, 61
Archaeopteryx, 42, 45, 61
armadillo, 23, 24
artificial selection, 30-31

B

bacteria, 48, 56, 61;
fossil, 26, 55, 60
bases (DNA), 52, 53, 55, 57
Bates, Henry, 25
bats, 22, 38, 42
bears, 39; cave, 8, 62;
polar, 35, 38
beetles, 21, 49;
bombardier, 43
Bible, 6, 10, 14, 16
birds, 12, 23, 25, 41, 47;
evolution, 42, 45, 62;
skeleton, 45
bryozoans, 60
Buckland, William, 18
Buffon, Georges, 40
Burgess shale, 47
butterflies, 13, 33, 41, 49

C

Cambrian period, 47, 60;
explosion, 26, 46
camouflage, 36, 58
Carboniferous period, 61
catastrophe theory, 16-17, 28
Cenoceras, 27
Cenozoic era, 47, 61, 62
Chalcides spp., 43
Chambers, Robert, 19
chromosomes, 51, 52
climate, 17, 38, 60, 63
coal, 11, 16, 44
coelacanth, 47
continental drift, 60-63
courtship rituals, 41
crab, hermit, 54;
Alaskan king, 54
creation, 6-7, 14, 16, 17
Cretaceous period, 61, 62
Crick, Francis, 52, 54
Curie, Pierre, 29
Cuvier, Georges, 15, 16, 17, 18, 28
cyanobacteria, 26, 56, 60

D

Darwin, Charles, 12, 19, 20-21, 22, 48;
adaptation, 24, 39, 42;
artificial selection, 30;
colonization, 25;
heredity, 33;
human evolution, 58;
natural selection, 28, 29, 34, 35, 36; sexual selection, 37; species, 40; variation, 32
Darwin, Erasmus, 21
Darwin, George, 29
Darwinism, 43, 50
da Vinci, Leonardo, 10
Devonian period, 60, 61
diluvialism, 10
dinosaurs, 15, 18-19, 26, 45, 61;
extinction, 46, 47, 62
Diplocaulus, 61
DNA, 31, 43, 51, 52-55;
mutation, 32;
origin, 56, 57
Dobzhansky, Theodosius, 41
dogs, 30, 31, 32
dolphin, 22, 23
dominant genes, 33, 51
donkey, 41, 48
double helix, 52, 53
dragonfly, 11, 49
Drosophila, 51

E

Ediacara fauna, 26, 47, 60
elephant, 8, 15, 54;
evolution, 44, 62
Enaliarctos, 44
Eozoon, 26, 27
Equus, 48
erosion, 16, 29
evolutionary tree, 48-49, 54
extinction, 14-15, 49, 63;
catastrophe theory, 16;
geological periods, 17

F

fertilization, 41, 50, 51
fish, armoured, 17, 60;
evolution, 61, 62;
flying, 42; fossil, 8, 47
flies, 49; fruit, 41, 51
flood, 10-11, 14, 16
fossils, 8-11, 14, 22, 56;
evidence, 26-27, 28, 55, 60; geological periods, 16, 17; intermediates, 42, 44-45, 46
Franklin, Rosalind, 52
frogs, 35, 44, 61

G

genes, 50, 51, 52, 57
genetic code, 47, 52, 55, 56
genetics, 41, 58
genus, 48
geological periods, 16, 17, 46, 61
Glyptodon, 24, 62
Goethe, Johann, 13
Gomphoceras, 27
Gould, Stephen Jay, 58
Grant, Professor Robert, 20
Gray, Asa, 42

H

Haeckel, Ernst, 48
heredity, 33, 50, 51, 52
Herodotus, 10
HMS *Beagle*, 20, 21
Homo erectus, 63
Hooker, Joseph, 24
horse, 23, 30, 41, 48, 62
humans, 15, 39;
evolution, 63
Huxley, Thomas H., 48
hybrids, 41, 50, 51
Hyracotherium, 48, 62

IJK

Ice Age, 8, 9, 17, 62, 63
Ichthyosaur, 18
Iguanodon, 18, 19, 61
inheritance, 13, 32-33, 36
insects, 11, 22, 25, 55;
evolution, 49, 61;
social, 58, 59
interbreeding, 22, 40
intermediates, 46, 47;
fossil, 26, 44-45;
living, 42-43
invertebrates, 46, 60
isolating mechanisms, 22, 40, 41
Jarvis, Jennifer, 59
Jefferson, Thomas, 14, 15
Jurassic period, 61
Kelvin, Lord, 29
Kimura, Motoo, 54

L

Lamarck, Jean-Baptiste de, 12-13, 16, 21, 32;
theory, 20, 33
Lamarckism, 12-13, 15, 58
Larus spp., 40
Littré, Maximilien, 58
Lyell, Charles, 17, 20, 28, 29
Lysenko, Trofim, 58

M

Malthus, Rev. Thomas, 34
mammal-like reptiles, 26, 61, 62
mammals, 25, 27, 30, 41, 46;
distribution, 24;
egg-laying, 42, 43;
evolution, 26, 47, 62-63;
genetic code, 55;
humans, 39;
limb, 22, 23, 38
mammoths, 17, 44, 54, 62
Mantell, Gideon 18, 19
mass extinctions, 16, 17, 46, 47, 61
mastodon, 14, 15, 44, 54, 62
Megalosaurus, 18
Megatherium, 14, 63
Mendel, Gregor, 33, 50-51, 58
Merychippus, 48
Mesohippus, 48
Mesozoic era, 46, 61
Miacis, 44
migration, 24, 40
Miller, Hugh, 17
Miller, Stanley, 57
molluscs, 26, 32, 55
Morgan, Thomas Hunt, 41, 51
moths, 41, 49;
peppered, 36, 58
mutation, 32, 36, 51, 52, 53, 54
Myophorella, 8

N

natural selection, 36-37, 43;
adaptation, 38, 39, 42;
competition, 32, 34, 35;
Darwin, 20, 22, 31, 33;
Mendelism, 50;
theories, 58
natural theology, 38, 39
nautiloids, 27, 60, 61
Nautilus, 9
Neanderthals, 63
Nerites, 32
Nollet, Jean Antoine, 12

OP

Ordovician period, 60
origin of life, 56-57, 60
Ornitholestes, 45
Orthoceras, 27
Owen, Richard, 18, 19
oxygen, 56, 57, 61
Palaeotherium, 62
Palaeozoic era, 46, 60, 61
Paley, Rev. William, 34, 38
Pasteur, Louis, 13
Peale, Charles Willson, 15
Permian period, 61
phenotype, 50
Phiomia, 44, 62
Phragmoceras, 27
plants, breeders, 31;
distribution, 24;
evolution, 61, 62;
selection, 30; sundew, 37; varieties, 50, 51
Pliny the Elder, 8, 9
Pliohippus, 48
Plot, Dr Robert, 8
pollination, 21, 22, 50
Precambrian, 26, 27, 47, 60, 61
Priestley, Joseph, 21
Proconsul, 62
Procynosuchus, 26, 27, 61
Pythagoras, 10

QR

Quaternary period, 62
Rafinesque, Constantine, 22
recessive genes, 33, 51
reptiles, 25, 27;
dinosaurs, 18;
evolution, 26, 43, 61
Ridersia, 26
RNA, 56, 57

S

Scheuzer, Johann, 10
sea-shells, 10, 11, 32
sedimentary rocks, 10, 11, 28
selective breeding, 30
sexual selection, 37
Silurian period, 46, 60
skeletons, hominid, 63;
mastodon, 15
skulls, cave bear, 9, 62;
elephant, 8; hominid, 63
sloth, giant ground, 14, 63;
two-toed, 23
Smith, William, 16, 17
species, 13, 36, 40-41;
fossil, 44; genus, 48;
natural selection, 22;
Sphenops sepsoides, 43
sponge, 9, 55
spontaneous generation, 13
Stensen, Niels, 9
Stephanoceras, 27
strata, 16, 17
struggle for existence, 32, 34-35, 36
subspecies, 13, 22, 40
synapsid opening, 26, 27

T

teeth, 14, 15, 17;
Archaeopteryx, 45;
Iguanodon, 18;
Procynosuchus, 27;
sabre-tooth tiger, 62;
shark, 9
Tennyson, Alfred Lord, 34, 35
Tertiary period, 47, 62
Tertullian, 10
Thompson, William, 28, 29
transitional fossils, 42
Triassic period, 46, 61
trilobites, 26, 46, 60
Tyrannosaurus, 61

UVW

uniformitarianism, 16, 17
variation, 32-33, 36, 50
vertebrae, 15, 62
vertebrates, 22, 23
Wallace, Alfred, 20, 36, 58
Watson, James, 52, 54
Wedgwood, Josiah, 21
Werner, Abraham, 16
White, Gilbert, 41

Acknowledgments

Dorling Kindersley would like to thank: Jeremy Adams, John Cooper and Gerald Legg at the Booth Museum, Hove; Solene Morris at Down House; Nick Arnold, Ian Bishop, David Carter, Sandra Chapman, Paul Clark, Andy Currant, Paul Hillyard, Jerry Hooker, Robert Kruszynski, David Lewis, Tim Parmenter, Alison Paul, David Reid, Lee Rogers and Sally Young at the Natural History Museum; Denise Blagden; Tom Kemp, Philip Powell, Monica Price and Derek Siveter at the Oxford University Museum; and Jack Challoner, for all their advice and help with the provision of objects for photography; Margaret Brown of the Medical Research Council, Cambridge; Chris Faulkes of the Institute of Zoology, London; and Jim Hamill at the British Museum (Ethnographic), for their help; Sarah Ashun, Jonathan Buckley, Jane Burton, Peter Chadwick, Philip Dowell, Andreas von Einsiedel, Frank Greenaway, Derek Hall, Colin Keates, Dave King, Karl Shone and Jerry Young for photography; Deborah Rhodes for page make-up. **DTP Manager** Joanna Figg-Latham. **Illustrations** Stephen Bull and Frazer May. **Index** Jane Parker.

Publisher's note No animal has been injured or harmed in any way during the preparation of this book.

For this edition, the publisher would also like to thank: consultant Kim Bryan for assisting with the updates; Lisa Stock for editorial assistance; David Ekholm-JAlbum, Sunita Gahir, Susan Malyan, Susan St Louis, Lisa Stock, and Bulent Yusuf for the clip art; Sue Nicholson and Edward Kinsey for the wall chart; Monica Byles and Stewart J Wild for proofreading; Margaret Parrish and John Searcy for Americanization.

Picture credits
The publisher would like to thank the following for their kind permission to reproduce their photographs:

(Key: a-above; b-below/bottom; c-center; f-far; l-left; r-right; t-top)

Alamy Images: blickwinkel / S. Gerth 71cra; David R. Frazier Photolibrary, Inc. 68l; The London Art Archive 64cla; Mary Evans Picture Library 66cr; PHOTOTAKE Inc. 67cra; Nick Turner 69clb. **American Museum of Natural History:** 65cl. **American Philosophical Society, Philadelphia:** 15bl. **Ancient Art and Architecture Collection:** 8br, 16br. **Bettmann Archive:** 50bl, 57bl. **The Bridgeman Art Library:** 20bl; Natural History Museum, London 64c. **British Library:** 7bl, 7bc. **British Museum:** 16bl. **Neil Bromhall:** 59cr; 59cl. **Brown Brothers:** 41br. **Camera Press:** 52bl, 58tr. **Bruce Coleman:** Stephen Bord 11 tr, 35tl; Pekka Hallor 39br, 43br; Hans Rheinard 53br; Konrad Wothe 47cr. **Corbis:** Dung Vo Trung / Politika 69bc. **DK Images:** Josef Hlasek 65cra (wood mouse); Mike Linley 65tc; Natural History Museum, London 64clb, 64-71 (background), 66cb, 69crb; Rough Guides 65tl, 68tr. **Chris Faulkes:** 59tr. **Getty Images:** Joseph Van Os / The Image Bank 71bc. **Giraudon:** 40tl. **Michael Holford:** 6bc, 30bl.
Hulton Deutsche Collection Ltd: 13tr, 13cr, 17cr, 21cl, 28tl, 36bc, 43tr, 54cr. **Illustrated London News Picture Library:** 30cr. **Mansell Collection:** 12tl, 14tl, 17tl, 19bl, 20cl, 21cr, 29tr, 33cl, 34tr, 36tl, 41cl, 42cl, 63br. **Mary Evans Picture Library:** 9bl, 10tl, 13br, 19cl, 25bc, 42-3c, 48cr, 56br, 61bl. **Professor Rory Mortimore, University of Brighton:** 11 cr. MRC Laboratory of Molecular Biology: 53l. **Natural History Museum Picture Library:** 12cr, 18cr,19tl, 24br, 25tc. **N.H.P.A.:** 38br; Philippa Scott 39cr, 42bl. **Oxford Scientific Films:** 35tr, 36cr. **Peale Museum, Baltimore:** 15cl. **Pennsylvania Academy of Fine Arts:** 14tr. **Planet Earth / Richard Coomber:** 39cl, 47tr. **Ann Ronan at Image Select:** 10bl, 50tl. **Department of Palaeontology, Royal Belgian Institute of Natural Sciences, Brussels:** 19tr. **Royal Society:** 19ct, 24tl, 29tl. **Science Museum Photo Library:** 7tr; Jean-Loup Charmet 16tl, 17bl, 29cl; Eric Grave 56cl; James King-Holmes 67br; NASA 29bc, 46cr, 50c, 50cb, 50br, 52cl, 58tl; Novosti 58bl; David Parker 54tl; Pasieka 70clb; Sinclair Stammers 56cr. **St Paul's Girls School:** 52tl. **By permission of the Syndics of Cambridge University Library:** 30cl. **Transylvania University Library, Special Collections, Kentucky:** 22tl. **Werner Foreman Archive:** 7tl. **Professor H. B. Whittington, University of Cambridge:** 46tl, 47tl, 60bl. **William Sturgis Bigelow Collection, Museum of Fine Arts, Boston:** 6tr. **Zefa:** 37cl, 49tr, 56tl.

Wall chart
DK Images: Booth Museum of Natural History, Brighton c (all butterflies, except 1st from right, 1st row), clb (grasshopper, stick insects and cockroach); The Home of Charles Darwin, Down House (English Heritage) / Natural History Museum, London cl (telescope and compass); Natural History Museum, London bc (flint hand axe), bl (skulls), br, ftr; **Getty Images:** fcla.

All other images © Dorling Kindersley
For further information see:
www.dkimages.com

AFRICA
AMERICAN REVOLUTION
AMPHIBIAN
ANCIENT CHINA
ANCIENT EGYPT
ANCIENT GREECE
ANCIENT ROME
ARCHEOLOGY
ARCTIC & ANTARCTIC
ARMS & ARMOR
ASTRONOMY
AZTEC, INCA & MAYA
BASEBALL
BASKETBALL
BATTLE
BIBLE LANDS
BIRD
BOAT
BOOK
BUDDHISM
BUILDING
BUTTERFLY & MOTH
CAR
CASTLE
CAT
CHEMISTRY
CHINA
CHRISTIANITY
CIVIL WAR
CLIMATE CHANGE
COSTUME
COWBOY
CRIME & DETECTION
CRYSTAL & GEM
DANCE
DA VINCI & HIS TIMES
DESERT
DINOSAUR
DOG
EAGLE & BIRDS OF PREY
EARLY HUMANS
EARTH
ECOLOGY
ECONOMY
ELECTRICITY
ELECTRONICS
ELEPHANT
ENERGY
EPIDEMIC
EVEREST
EVOLUTION
EXPLORER
FARM
FILM
FIRST LADIES
FISH
FLAG
FLYING MACHINE
FOOD
FOOTBALL
FORCE & MOTION
FORENSIC SCIENCE
FOSSIL
FUTURE
GORILLA, MONKEY & APE
GOYA
GREAT MUSICIANS
GREAT SCIENTISTS
HORSE
HUMAN BODY
HURRICANE & TORNADO
IMPRESSIONISM
INDIA
INSECT
INVENTION
ISLAM
JUDAISM
JUNGLE
KNIGHT
LIFE
LIGHT
MAMMAL
MANET
MARS
MATTER
MEDIA & COMMUNICATION
MEDICINE
MEDIEVAL LIFE
MESOPOTAMIA
MONET